The New Testament
in Contemporary Life

Virgil Thompson

Gonzaga University

Kendall Hunt
publishing company

Cover images © 2011 Shutterstock, Inc.

Kendall Hunt
publishing company

www.kendallhunt.com
Send all inquiries to:
4050 Westmark Drive
Dubuque, IA   52004-1840

Copyright © 2012 by Kendall Hunt Publishing Company

ISBN 978-0-7575-9764-0

Printed in the United States of America
10   9   8   7   6   5   4   3   2

Table of Contents

FOREWORD

Roy A. Harrisville
Professor Emeritus of New Testament

Walter Sundberg
Professor of Church History
Luther Seminary

According to its author, Virgil Thompson, New Testament lecturer at Gonzaga University in Spokane, Washington, the purpose of this volume is to "prepare students to hear the 'voice' of the New Testament in the context of contemporary life" (see Introduction). Clearly, the purpose is not to compete on a professional level with the thousand and one disquisitions on the New Testament, but to introduce the American college student to a body of literature with which he/she may have had absolutely no, or little, prior acquaintance.

Following the introduction, this "study guide," as its author calls it, is comprised of five parts, the first of which deals with the question: "What is the New Testament?" The professional or guild member will readily recognize the customary review of the New Testament documents, but it may never have occurred to the student that the documents represent several genres; each writing represents a reconstruction from evidence at second-hand, and the gathering of the Gospels, Epistles and Apocalypse into a "canon" was an event independent of ecclesiastical decree.

Since, as Thompson puts it, from beginning to end the New Testament qualifies as the "subject matter of theology," chapter two deals with the question: "What is Theology?" Following a brief review of the entanglement of Christian theology with Greek thought, the student is introduced to two classical approaches to the question, the approach of Ignatius of Loyola and of Martin Luther. Contending that neither would have a bone to pick with Plato and Aristotle respecting the place of reason in the articulation of faith, Thompson proceeds to contrast Luther's understanding of theological existence as passive with Ignatius's understanding of it as active toward reshaping the self.

Chapter three deals with "The New Testament as Literature." Here, our author is clearly warming to his subject. Learning to read the Bible as literature, Thompson contends, will assist students in unlearning old approaches, make them aware of the various interpretive decisions involved in giving voice to the text, and offer an approach that leads to a "respectful, rich, and sensitive encounter with the Word of the New Testament." Thus, the most promising way by which to encounter the New Testament is to read it as literature. Such a reading involves seeing the New Testament writings through the lens of the situation of their first recipients, in light of the forms and logic used in their composition, and giving attention to the ways in which the stories of Jesus and the early church create a "narrative world" into which the readers are drawn. Along the way, the reader is cautioned to respect authorial ascription, referred to the "implied" author as can be inferred from the piece itself, and to the crucial status of the narrator. Acknowledging that in such a reading, historical considerations, narrative analysis, and rhetorical and theological considerations will be in play, the literary approach promises to enrich the encounter with the various types that comprise the collection.

In chapter four, Thompson deals with "The New Testament as History." In the first part of the chapter he clarifies what asking and answering the question respecting the historical integrity of the New Testament involves, and in the second part contextualizes the New Testament in the historical world of its day. It is here that Thompson finds Paul Ricoeur's suggestions regarding the world **behind** the text, **of** the text, and **in front of** the text, helpful in structuring historical inquiry. The chapter concludes with a review of the historical context of earliest Christianity and its separation from Rabbinic Judaism.

To chapter five, "The New Testament as Rhetorical Speech," our author gives most attention. He argues that the power of the New Testament to shape and move readers is not exhausted by the rhetorical style of its authors. He concedes that the literary and historical approaches to the material are indispensable. Nevertheless, exclusive use of the historical approach could give the impression that the message of the New Testament is to be located in the past, and such use of the literary approach could give the impression that interpretation involves uncovering what is hidden in the text. A rhetorical approach, on the other hand, regards literature as a force. It views the New Testament "not only as a message about God, but as the very speech of God." Thus, if the literary, historical, and rhetorical approaches enjoy a complementarity, the rhetorical approach overarches.

In contemporary reading of the New Testament, advocates of the rhetorical approach are usually loath to give space to historical inquiry, thus tend to accent the text's inherent ambiguity. In a line become classical, Frank Kermode writes of our "sole hope and pleasure" as the "perception of a momentary radiance, before the door of disappointment is finally shut on us."[1] For all his enjoyment of classical and contemporary accent on the text as persuasion, Thompson will not concede it a mere "momentary radiance." The reason why is that for the college or university student, the question, "did it really happen?" does not go away. The attraction of Aristotle's *Poetics*, and all those in its train—the elusive Longinus, William Wordsworth, Matthew Arnold, Samuel Taylor Coleridge—is tempered by a taste for historical inquiry into the text with its "three worlds."

One final note: Thompson is a superb pedagogue. He is patient as he unfolds his arguments; he goes step by step, providing accurate and uncluttered definitions of all specialized vocabulary essential to the disciplines of biblical theology and biblical studies. The reader always knows where he or she is in chapter and page. This quality of clarity

---

[1]Frank Kermode, *The Genesis of Secrecy: On the Interpretation of Narrative* (Cambridge: Harvard University Press, 1979), 145.

that pervades the work no doubt comes from years of experience in the college class-room where, in the matter of religion generally and Christianity specifically, no teacher can assume any familiarity with the subject matter on the part of students. Ours is an increasingly secular society, especially for members of the millennial generation who in-habit our colleges and universities today. A teacher in a religion department, who wants to be constructive and not destructive or cynical with regard to matters of faith, takes on an apologetic task of the first order. Thompson is a constructive teacher, one who builds up and does not tear down. For the experienced reader who knows biblical studies and theology, Thompson's clarity makes for the type of intellectual pleasure that can be got-ten from a good handbook or encyclopedia article: that is, a laying out of the fundamen-tals which one knows or thinks one knows or used to know, but is now seen afresh. To these fundamentals Thompson brings an original mind, putting things in a new way that makes the book a genuine contribution to the field.

Introduction

Not surprisingly, over the course of the centuries the New Testament as one division of the **Christian Scriptures** has informed and shaped Christian imagination in many respects. One could scarcely imagine a public worship service of the church that did not prominently feature readings from the New Testament. It would be even more difficult to imagine understanding the Christian view of God, faith, and life apart from the New Testament. The New Testament, along with the Old Testament, is so central to the life of the Christian community not only because it contains information about God and human life in relation to God. Christians believe that by means of the Bible God speaks to create and sustain the life of the community of faith. Christians read the Bible expecting to hear the lively Word of God. The expectation arises out of the promise of Jesus, "the Holy Spirit, whom the Father will send in my name, will teach you everything, and remind you of all that I have said to you" (John 14:26; see also John 16:13–15).[1] Christians believe that Scripture is the means by which God continues to speak in order to create and sustain the life of faith.

The influence of the New Testament is not, however, limited to the four walls of the church. In part, at least, the New Testament has informed and shaped the cultural imagination of the world—east and west. People whose education has included study of the Bible will hear echoes of its speech in the ordinary language of today. Consider for example everyday expressions like, "labor of love," "Ye of Little Faith," "A voice crying in the wilderness," "woe is me," "wolf in sheep's clothing," "Chariot of Fire," "thorn in the flesh," "turn the other cheek," "spare the rod, spoil the child," "do unto others as you would have them do unto you," "salt of the earth," "sheep to the slaughter," "let there be light," "the meek shall inherit the earth," "a fly in the ointment," "a drop in the bucket," "walks on water," "by the skin of your teeth," "an eye for an eye," "on the straight and narrow," "go the extra mile," "the hand writing is on the wall," "you reap what you sow," and "ashes to ashes, dust to dust." All of these expressions, and many more, come from the Bible.

As well, images and symbols of the Bible have frequently found their way into American political rhetoric. Presidents Kennedy and Reagan, for example, referred to the United States as a "city upon a hill." In his "Farewell Address to the Nation," January 11, 1989, President Reagan explained what he meant—"in my mind it was a tall, proud city built on rocks stronger than oceans, windswept, God-blessed, and teeming

---

[1]Unless otherwise noted, biblical quotations come from The HarperCollins Study Bible, revised edition, edited by Harold W. Attridge (San Francisco: Harper Collins Publishers, 2006).

with people of all kinds living in harmony and peace."[2] Historians trace the image to a seventeenth-century sermon of the founding father, John Winthrop. It did not however originate with Winthrop. It comes from the Bible. To be specific the image comes from Jesus's Sermon on the Mount in Matthew 5.

In twentieth-century America without doubt the most eloquent and powerful use of Christian Scripture by a civic leader may be found in the sermons and speeches of Martin Luther King Jr., the civil rights leader. Biblical language and imagery are woven into the fabric of his rhetoric. In fact, the power of his rhetoric is practically synonymous with the power of biblical language. As J. Louis Martyn has shown, Dr. King's rhetoric contrasts two kinds of power, the conditional power of coercion and the unconditional power of grace. The vision which animated Martin Luther King and the civil rights movement was not contingent upon anything. The biblical vision prophetically announces what is promised by the unilateral decision of God. "Not *if* you repent. Not *if* you learn. Not even *if* you believe. In the absence of that little word *if*, the uncontingent, prevenient, invading nature of God's grace shows God to be the powerful and victorious Advocate who is intent on the liberation of the entire race of human beings. This is the victorious power that one saw in Birmingham and in Montgomery."[3] It is also the power of biblical language.

The Bible casts a long shadow not only over everyday speech and political rhetoric. Its language, images, and symbols permeate our poetry, music, visual art, theater, and fiction. You may be familiar with explicit portrayals of the biblical story in film and musical theater, such as *Godspell* and *Jesus Christ Superstar*. More often biblical themes and allusions show up more subtly in literature and film. But people familiar with the Bible see its influence from *The Simpsons* to *The Terminator*. Occasionally the Bible even makes an appearance on the theatrical stage. On the occasion of the 400th anniversary of the King James Bible the Bush Theater in London commissioned and produced "Sixty-Six Books," a series of theatrical reflections on each book of the Bible. As Jeanette Winterson, one of the playwrights observes, "The Bible is problematic but never dull, unless you are in church."[4] It is an observation that the church might take to heart and perhaps the university too.

Such examples illustrate the undeniable influence of the New Testament in shaping our culture, expression, and imagination. As the scholar of culture, Northrop Frye, says, "this huge, sprawling, tactless book sit[s] there inscrutably in the middle of our cultural heritage, frustrating all our efforts to walk around it."[5] Given its interest in themes so central to human life—revenge and forgiveness, right and wrong, worthiness and unworthiness, love and hate, sex, greed and generosity, passion and apathy toward life, ending and beginnings, to say nothing of its defining interest in the Christian God—it's not surprising, artists, composers, writers, moral educators, and political and religious lead-

---

[2] Text is from The American President Project – online at http://www.presidency.ucsb.edu/ws/index.php?pid=29650#axzz1tolQXwWm
[3] J. Louis Martyn, *Theological Issues in the Letters of Paul* (Nashville: Abingdon Press, 1997), 289.
[4] Patrick Healy, "At London Theater, a Celebration of Biblical Proportions," *New York Times*, October 24, 2011, p. C1, 6.
[5] Quoted from Northrop Frye, *The Great Code: The Bible and Literature* (London: Routledge & Kegan Paul, 1982), pp. xviii–xix, in John Barton, *The Bible: the basics* (London: Routledge, 2010), 17.

ers have found themselves engaged with the Bible. About that there can be no question. One might question, however, whether the people of today will continue to recognize the influence of the New Testament, let alone, engage its message. It is remarkable to me that some of the most public voices on the question of God in contemporary life—whether negative or positive—are uninformed by the biblical story of God. As the Gospel writer Mark might suggest, a contemporary encounter with the biblical God would likely result in the same reversal as humanity suffered in the encounter with Jesus. Those on the inside found themselves on the outside and those on the outside found themselves on the inside (see, e.g., Mark 2:17).

Whether the New Testament will continue to have a place in contemporary imagination cannot be said ahead of time. It depends upon what happens to each generation of readers in the actual encounter with the writings that comprise the collection. As one of my teachers has said,

> Ultimately, the authority of the Bible stems from its self-authentication in the heart and mind of believers. At bottom, the Scriptures of Old and New Testaments derive their authority . . . from their power to evoke assent and trust, to wring a "yes! yes!" from deep inside their readers and hearers . . .[6]

What happens in the actual encounter with the New Testament will determine not only whether the New Testament has a place in contemporary life but what sort of place it will have. In what ways and to what extent will the New Testament shape contemporary theological[7] imagination? No book, except the "book" of the New Testament itself, can decide such questions. Only the actual encounter will determine what comes of it.

Encountering God in the Encounter with the New Testament

The encounter with the New Testament has been compared to entering a "strange new land."[8] Traveling in new lands can be exciting, enriching, even life-changing. It can also be bewildering and disorienting. Students, who have had little or no prior exposure to the New Testament writings, often report their uncertain expectation. The reflection of this student is typical.

> My family is not religious. I did not attend private school, nor was our family active in the church. When I learned that I had to take a college course on the Bible I did not

---

[6] Roy Harrisville, "The Loss of the Biblical Authority and Its Recovery," in *Reclaiming the Bible for the Church*, edited by Carl E. Braaten and Robert W. Jenson (Grand Rapids: Eerdmans, 1995), 48.

[7] Like any academic discipline the study of the New Testament has a special vocabulary. One of the objectives of this guide to reading the New Testament is to familiarize students with these terms as they arise in the course of things. For our immediate purposes we may say that theological imagination refers to the way in which we imagine the relationship between God and humans. In the chapter devoted to the theological nature of the New Testament and the academic discipline of theology we will develop more fully, understanding related to theology.

[8] Karl Barth, "The Strange New World within the Bible," in *The Word of God and the Word of Man* (Gloucester: Peter Smith, 1978), 28–50.

know what to expect. I wondered what the study of the New Testament could contribute to my education. I also thought that everyone would be far more advanced in their understanding. I am finding, however, as we get into the course that the homework assignments prepare me to enter the discussion on the same level as my classmates. Also, I find our discussions of the New Testament more interesting than I could have imagined at the outset.

Even students who have had prior exposure to the New Testament quickly discover that their first university course in the study of the New Testament opens up, unexpectedly, new vistas on these old writings and the issues at their heart. As one student recently observed,

> Overall this course has expanded my "grade-school/high-school" familiarity with the New Testament. For example, when you said that we were going to read Mark's Gospel I thought, "Oh, no, I can't take it. For me the 'new' went out of the New Testament long ago." But when I began to see how Mark works as a story it opened up a whole new world on the question of God. The world of God as portrayed by Mark is far more interesting than I was previously led to believe, but also scarier.

This study guide has both students in mind. It provides the means of engaging the New Testament in a constructive and fruitful way. It aims to prepare students to hear the "voice" of the New Testament text in the context of contemporary life. I am completely in agreement with my teacher, Donald Juel, when he says, "I can imagine no sound reason for interest in study of the Bible if it does not provide for more lively engagement with the material."[9] If our course of study does not produce more engaged readers then it is a waste of time. Such an ambition involves us in a tricky enterprise.

On the one hand, the reality is, at least on one level, that to "hear" the voice of the text readers must "give" voice to the text. The text of the New Testament is just words on the page. The words have no voice until readers give them voice. Of course the New Testament can be read without the support of a university course. But if readers want to hear the voice of the text for what it is a university course can be helpful. It can provide the opportunity for readers to cultivate historical and linguistic knowledge that contributes to the experience of hearing the text on its own terms. Of course, to be honest about it, university study of the Bible could also amount to a sophisticated exercise in taking the voice of the New Testament captive to the contemporary prejudices and agendas of its interpreters—conservative or liberal. A genuine encounter with the New Testament proves that God refuses to be domesticated by human agendas. As Mark declares in his story of Jesus, God comes "tearing out of heaven and into human life" with an agenda of God's own (Mark 1:10). How the encounter with the God of the Bible may turn out cannot be said ahead of time, but it likely will not leave you the same. Leander Keck, a prominent biblical scholar, sees promise in plumbing the depths of the lived experience of the Bible to learn "what is important, life-giving, and emancipating in it." If, however,

---

[9]Don Juel, *A Master of Surprise* (Minneapolis: Fortress, 1994), 6.

the promise is to be realized, he continues, "nothing can replace reading the text again and again, questioning and being questioned, objecting and being objected to, discovering and being discovered."[10]

The Challenge of an Introduction to the Encounter

The challenge of an introductory study guide to reading the New Testament involves strategic decisions regarding how much beginning students need to know in order to engage the text and their class colleagues in theological conversation that is actually consequential for life. Knowledge about the Bible completely overwhelms even the professional scholar. Interest in and study of the Bible has generated mountains of secondary literature. No one person could keep abreast of every development. More to the point, introductions to the Bible by experts in the field frequently smother the student with all there is to know. So overwhelmed with the acquisition of introductory knowledge about the Bible, students have little time and energy to enter into sustained engagement with the God of the Bible. A good introduction will strike a balance between too little and too much. What background knowledge—historical, rhetorical, literary, and theological— actually enriches contemporary engagement with the Bible as the Word of God? Take, as just one example, the place of historical background in the study of the Bible.

The New Testament writings were produced from the perspective of Jewish experience in the Greco-Roman world of the first century. To hear these writings in their own voice requires us, in a disciplined way, to expand our imaginations, historically and linguistically. This is not easy. Without awareness we tend, automatically, to take in everything through the lens of our own culture, socio-economic position, gender, language, and religious sensibility. We always face the danger of hearing only the voice of our own outlook imposed upon the text, forcing the text into expression of our own prejudices. No doubt it comforts us to hear the familiar voice of our convictions. But we gain nothing by reducing the New Testament to a "mini-me." Respecting the historical distance between contemporary life and antiquity promises to make audible the New Testament in its own voice. Note, however, I said that historical study *promises* to make audible the New Testament in its own voice. There are no guarantees that a historical approach to reading the New Testament will save us from reducing the New Testament to a "mini-me." Historical method can be used to front interpretative prejudices just as well as helping us see them more clearly. As the Danish philosopher Søren Kierkegaard has observed, disciplined studies of the Bible, including historical study, may be used to defend "oneself against God's Word."[11] But it may also be the means by which readers come to life in the promise of Jesus. Either way, historical inquiry promises to help us hear the New Testament in its own voice.

---

[10]"The Premodern Bible in the Postmodern World." *Interpretation* 50.2 (1996): 135.

[11]Quoted in Edgar Krentz, *The Historical-Critical Method* (Philadelphia: Fortress Press, 1975), 3; originally from Søren Kierkegaard, *For Self-Examination and Judge for Yourselves and Three Discourses, 1851.* Translated by Walter Lowrie (Princeton: Princeton University Press, 1944), 56.

But just as soon as we make the case for the indispensability of historical studies we face the danger of Bible study that never gets out of the ancient world. Imagining how the New Testament was heard by previous generations is not an end in itself. Our study aims to hear the New Testament in contemporary life. Our interest in history serves that aim. Too often contemporary study of the Bible in the university has been content to leave the text at the safe distance of what it might have meant long, long ago in a place far, far away. Students never hear the voice of the Bible in the context of their own lives. So the trick is to manage the historical approach so that it serves to enrich engagement with what the biblical text has to say to our own time and place in life. We will have more to say about this aspect of things in the chapter on the place of historical study in the contemporary encounter with the New Testament writings. For the moment we seek to drive home the point that hearing the New Testament in its own voice involves the expansion of historical background knowledge—along with literary, rhetorical, and theological knowledge.

Taking the Challenge

So then to put a point on our challenge: Too much knowledge and the wrong kind of knowledge can be suffocating. Not enough knowledge leaves us vulnerable to merely reading our own voice into and over top of the text. In these pages I share what I have learned over the years from, and with, my teachers, colleagues, and students. Together we have read, pondered, discussed, and debated what to make of the New Testament. In these discussions it has often seemed that the tables have been turned on us. Instead of discussing what to make of the New Testament we have found ourselves discussing what the New Testament makes of us. In any case, these discussions have served to enrich the contemporary encounter with the New Testament as Word of God. In preparing this study guide I have trimmed away the fat to provide a lean introduction that moves students directly into rich engagement with the writings of the New Testament. Each chapter of the study guide suggests further readings by which students may continue to pursue study of the New Testament as Word of God.

The New Testament is Truth to Tell

The title of the collection of writings which comprise the New Testament provides a promising place to begin our study. Thinking about the title of the collection provides us the opportunity to address the question: Why bother reading the New Testament? What is the New Testament good for?

Normally scholars explain that **testament**, because of its close association with **covenant**, appropriately names our collection of writings. Such scholars point out that covenant means agreement. In the Jewish Scriptures (a collection of writings roughly the same as the Christian Old Testament) the **Mosaic Covenant**, for example, names the agreement that Moses mediated between God and the people of Israel. Essentially the people agree to live by God's ordinances and God promises to take care of the people of Israel on the condition that they obey his commandments (see, e.g., Deut. 7:7–11). According to this view the followers of Jesus understood themselves to be the recipients of a new covenant which God has made with the people of Israel through Jesus (Jer. 31:31–34).

A minority of scholars—taking their cue from the insight of Martin Luther, a sixteenth-century theologian and biblical scholar—explain the title of the New Testament differently. Given the nature of the New Testament witness to God, this minority report seems more apropos to me. It reasons that in ordinary conversation we use the word **testament** in two ways. Both uses inform the way in which the name applies to these writings.

1) In a court of law, "testimony" refers to telling the truth. In that sense the term asserts that these writings tell the truth about God and humans. The truth that the writings tell is grounded in and arises out of the death and resurrection of Jesus of Nazareth. That singular event sets off all these writings. As the angel declared to the shepherds, Jesus is "good news for all people . . . a Savior, who is the Messiah, the Lord" (Luke 2:10–11). In the pages of New Testament the **apostles**[12] testify to the good news of Jesus for human life. In brief, this good news turns popular religious belief upside down. The apostle Paul for instance sees in the death and resurrection of Jesus the basis to believe that God declares himself unconditionally for the ungodly. As he puts it, "Christ died for the ungodly . . . God proves his love for us in that while we still were sinners Christ died for us . . . If while we were enemies, we were reconciled to God through the death of his Son, much more surely, having been reconciled will we be saved by his life" (Rom. 5:6, 8, 10). The Gospel writer John portrays Jesus as the God the world has never known (John 1:18). This God has come down in the person of Jesus and entered into our rough and tumble world to give life and to give it abundantly (John 10:10). For the writers of the New Testament the news of Jesus turns their world upside down. Whether the truth of Jesus will turn the world of contemporary readers upside down remains to be seen.

2) In that sense the other common usage of testament also applies to these writings. The other context in which contemporary people encounter the word testament is in "last will and testament." In the "last will and testament" people declare what should become of their personal property after they die. Death, so to speak, triggers the execution of one's will. In that sense the New Testament views the significance of Jesus's death and resurrection. His death executes the disposition of his will, which by his resurrection he lives to oversee. What Jesus dispenses in death is not property but himself. As he says at the Last Supper, " 'This is my body that is for you. Do this in remembrance of me.' In the same way he took the cup also, after supper, saying, 'This cup is the new *testament* in

---

[12]Apostle is best understood to mean, sent to speak with the full authority of the sender. This was precisely the meaning of Jesus when he appointed his twelve disciples as his apostles (see Mark 9:27 and parallels, also John 20:21). Frequently the New Testament itself is referred to as the apostolic witness to Jesus. Accordingly the New Testament is understood to be the earliest "authorized" witness to Jesus.

my blood. Do this as often as you drink it in remembrance of me'" (1 Cor. 11:23–25; my translation). He gives himself for the life of humanity. Strange as it may seem to say, Jesus was dying to give life: "Those who eat my flesh and drink my blood abide in me, and I in them . . . whoever eats me will live because of me" (John 6:56, 57b).

The declaration of the last will and testament cannot be changed after the testator has died. Just so, the death of Jesus executes the testament of God's will toward the believer. In other words, the New Testament gives voice to the final, decisive judgment of God toward creation, especially, toward God's human creatures. Listen to the way in which Jesus speaks about those who belong to him by baptism. "I give them eternal life, and they will never perish. No one will snatch them out of my hand. What my Father has given me is greater than all else, and no one can snatch it out of the Father's hand. The Father and I are one" (John 10:28–30). Unpacking the meaning and significance of the unconditional promise of God for human life is the project that lies before author and reader as this study guide leads us more deeply into the truth of God as we encounter it within the world of the New Testament writings.

Our Approach to the Encounter

This study guide takes a four-fold approach to reading the New Testament. In the first place, because the New Testament is words on the page our approach self-consciously takes account of *literary* considerations. Secondly, in as much as the particular words on the pages of the New Testament were written a long time ago and in a culture very different from our own culture and time, our approach takes into account *historical* considerations. Thirdly, we assume that like other authors, the authors of the New Testament seek to shape and move their readers to think and act in certain ways. Even more important, not only do the original authors seek to shape their readers but interpreters also seek to shape the experience of those with whom they read and converse. More important still, not only the original authors and contemporary interpreters but the Lord God as well seeks to create and shape the community of readers. Thus *rhetorical* analysis, inasmuch as it seeks to understand how readers are shaped in the encounter with a literary text, also informs our study of the New Testament. Finally, because these materials are fundamentally preoccupied with the question of God and human life in relation to God, our approach takes into account *theological* considerations. Throughout the course of our encounter with the New Testament we will strategically introduce and flesh out what is involved in each of these **methods**.[13] We will, as well, show the way they work together toward enriching the encounter with the New Testament as Word of God.

---

[13]Method as the roots of the word imply—*met* (along) *hod* (road)—provides a way for readers to make their way together along the same path into the heart of what they are reading.

The Aim of the Study

Paul Ricoeur's observation that texts exist simultaneously in three worlds helps to keep in focus the aim of this study guide. According to Ricoeur, texts—including the text of the New Testament—exist simultaneously in three worlds. He spoke of these worlds in terms of the world behind the text, the world of the text, and the world in front of the text.

The World of the Text

When applied to the New Testament the ***world of the text*** refers to the way in which the words on the page function to set forth an argument or weave a narrative. When reading the letters of the New Testament interpretation seeks to track and reconstruct the author's argument. When reading the Gospels, Acts, and Revelation the world of the text refers primarily to the narrative world as the author has constructed it. Interpretation seeks to reconstruct on the basis of the ***data***[14] provided by the author what happens, within the story world of the text, to whom, where, when, why, and how. The reconstruction of the narrative world or the argument of the text is essentially a literary enterprise. With respect to narratives, for example, readers can ask: Is it true that within Mark's story Jesus walks on water? As a literary question the evidence compels interpretation to answer in the affirmative. We have literary evidence, words on the page; his disciples "saw him walking on the sea," the narrator tells us (Mark 6:49). There can be no disputing that within the world of Mark's story Jesus walks on water.

Interpretive discourse promises to be most fruitful when it begins with the reconstruction of the narrative world. Before interpreters can discuss the significance of a narrative or textual argument first they must determine what occurs within the narrative world of the text. To the beginning student the task of reconstructing the world of the text may seem rather straightforward. My experience in the classroom suggests, to the contrary, that reconstructing what occurs in the story world of the text turns out to be much more challenging than one might at first imagine. Students frequently discover, to their surprise, in the story of the Bible a world as complex as contemporary life.

---

[14]Data refers to the words on the page along with the grammar, conventions, and devices employed by the author in the telling of the story.

For a variety of reasons reconstructing the world of the text requires work. Through-out the course of the semester we will devote our energies to this work. Like most work it will require the acquisition and cultivation of certain skills. Chapter three of this study guide brings into focus the literary aspect of making our way in the world of the New Testament.

The World Behind the Text

In addition to the world of the text interpretation also takes an interest in the **world behind the text**. The world behind the text as it applies to the New Testament has a two-fold reference. As Edgar Krentz explains, the writings of the New Testament "have a history that must be set into the framework of Israelite and nascent Christian history. The Bible also narrates a history, which, of course lies at an earlier stage than the books themselves. Both aspects must be investigated and used in the writing of the narrative account of Israel, Jesus, or the primitive church."[15]

So then, in the first place, the New Testament writings report events that ostensibly have taken place in the world of real time. For example, Luke reports that Jesus of Naza-reth was born when Augustus was emperor of the Roman Empire and Quirinius was governor of Syria (Luke 2:1–2). Readers want to know: Can we trust that the world of the text accurately reports what actually took place in the world of real time? Answering such questions requires interpretation to work with the rules of evidence as they are ap-plied by historians to the reconstruction of any past era.

The traffic of historical method also works the other way around. Readers of the New Testament will not understand the world which it depicts apart from expanding our background knowledge of Jewish life in the Greco-Roman world of the first century. For example, Mark's story of Jesus prominently features the Temple in Jerusalem. Nowhere in the story, however, does Mark explicitly describe the significance of the institution for first-century Jews. Presumably, it was unnecessary for Mark to describe the nature and significance of the Temple because his first-century audience had first-hand familiarity with its significance. Readers today however must work to expand our background knowledge to acquire understanding that would have been common place among Mark's first-century readers. The expansion of such background knowledge requires the cultiva-tion of historical imagination. While contemporary readers may never understand as fully as the first-century readers of the New Testament some things can be known. Knowing however will require us to work at developing some effective research skills and tools.

Using the New Testament text to reconstruct the world of depicted events in real time does not however exhaust interpretative interest in the world behind the text. Mark's Gospel, for instance, was composed at least forty years following the depicted events. Interpretation seeks to understand how the real world circumstances of Mark and his first audience have shaped the telling of Jesus's story.

---

[15]Edgar Krentz, *The Historical-Critical Method* (Philadelphia: Fortress Press, 1975), 37.

The World In Front of the Text

Finally, and ultimately, interpretation of the New Testament focuses attention on **the world in front of the text**, the world of contemporary readers. Does the New Testament say anything worthwhile to readers of today? Does the New Testament have a place in contemporary life, and if so, what sort of place does it have? What sort of place should it have? Again, no one can decide ahead of time the answers to such questions. The answers can only be made out in the actual encounter with the New Testament writings.

Of course, before the New Testament is read and interpreted in our world, it has been read and interpreted by readers in every era reaching back to the first readers contemporaneous with its production. Each of these generations of readers has left its fingerprints on the text. Each generation of readers has influenced the next generation of readers. Even if you have never read the New Testament for yourself, still, chances are quite high that you have been influenced in your view of the New Testament by the opinion of other readers, present as well as past. We read always in the light of other readings and as members of communities who share certain convictions, values, and outlooks.

The Influence of Interpretative Prejudice

The critical methods which have been briefly described and which will be more fully developed in the following pages have been in evolutionary development for the past two hundred and fifty years or so. They are designed to illuminate the process by which readers "give voice" to texts. While critical methods may open up vast new horizons on our understanding of the Bible, they do not insulate readers from personal response to the New Testament. Rather than imagining that critical method can bracket out personal response, it seems more honest, and more interesting, to acknowledge the reality that interpreters operate with interpretative prejudice, which is shaped by experience as well as by the communities to which we belong. Joel Green recalls the observation of Hans-Georg Gadamer who insisted "that we bring with us always and everywhere ourselves— our presuppositions and histories, our stories."[16] Our prior experiences, convictions, and home community, give us identity and provide the lens through which we make sense of and interact with the world, including the world of the New Testament. Of course presuppositions, prior experiences, and convictions can also work the other way around. They can blind us to the reality in front of our eyes. Seeing things for what they are, not only poses the challenge of reading the Bible, it is the challenge of life.

Throughout the Bible from Genesis to Revelation readers encounter many stories about seeing and not seeing, hearing and not hearing. There is, for example, a beautiful story in the final chapter of Luke's Gospel about two disciples who meet up with the risen Jesus. However, they fail to recognize him, until he opens their eyes by opening the

---

[16] Joel B. Green, *Seized by the Truth: Reading the Bible as Scripture* (Nashville: Abingdon Press, 2007), 24. This insight comes from the seminal work of Hans-Georg Gadamer, *Truth and Method* (New York: Crossroad, 1990).

Scriptures. Imagine that this remains the promise of reading the Bible. Where and when it pleases God to do it, the Spirit of Truth will open eyes to see things, truthfully, for what they are (John 14:18–31; 16:5–15).

In this aspect of things the old classical interpreters have much to teach modern readers. As Jane P. Tompkins has pointed out, "Classical commentaries on literature . . . exhibit an overwhelming preoccupation with audience response. Plato, Aristotle, Horace, and Longinus all discuss literature primarily in terms of its effects upon an audience."[17] From their point of view literature is to be appreciated as a force exerted upon the world. This ancient insight provides the focus for our study. Our aim is to understand the power of the New Testament literature to create worlds and shape realties. Ultimately the focus of study can be set forth in the question: What happens, or what should happen, to readers in the encounter with the New Testament?

The value of this study guide, like the proof of the pudding, will be in the tasting of the biblical message. Of course if the preoccupation with method and background were never to get beyond itself, the project would be something like reading travel guides but never going on the trip. As travel guides are for traveling, so this study guide is for a richer encounter with the biblical text. The study guide provides a convenient source of resources from which to draw in the course of reading the New Testament. The insights and methods offered by the study guide will be introduced, strategically, over the course of the student's engagement with the writings of the New Testament.

Understanding

Like any course in the university this course is designed and undertaken to expand student understanding of its subject matter. Understanding is difficult both to define and to measure. Taking their cue from David Perkins, who defines understanding as the "ability to think and act flexibly with what one knows," educational theorists, Grant Wiggins and Jay McTighe, take a performance-based approach to the question. For our purposes we have adopted and adapted their six signs of understanding.[18] Understanding is reflected in the ability . . .

1. . . . to **explain** (provide thorough, supported, and justifiable accounts of phenomena, facts, <u>data</u>).

2. . . . to **interpret** (tell meaningful stories; offer apt translations; provide a revealing historical or personal dimension to <u>ideas</u> and events; make it personal or accessible through images, anecdotes, analogies, and models).

3. . . . to **transfer** (effectively <u>use and adapt</u> what we know in diverse contexts).

---

[17]Jane P. Tompkins, "The Reader in History," *Reader Response Criticism*. Edited by Jane P. Tompkins. (Baltimore: The John Hopkins University Press, 1980), 202.

[18]Adapted from: *Understanding by Design*, Grant Wiggins and Jay McTighe (Columbus, OH: Merrill Prentice Hall, 1998).

4. . . . to **perceive** (see and hear points of view <u>through critical eyes and ears</u>; see the big picture)

5. . . . to **empathize** (capacity to experience feelings, thoughts, and attitudes of others; see sensitively on the basis of prior experience).

6. . . . for **self-knowledge** (perceive the personal style, prejudices, projections, and habits of mind, which both shape and impede understanding and which account, in part, for why understanding is so hard).

Terms:

Like all academic disciplines, theology and biblical studies have a special vocabulary. Each chapter of the study guide draws attention to important terms, highlighted in bold print and defined in the Glossary of Terms which you will find in Appendix A: Glossary of Terms (see pages 119–126 of this study guide).

Study Questions:

1. Which of the students, quoted on pages 3 and 4 of this chapter, do you most identify with? How do you imagine that your outlook at the outset of the course will affect your participation? What would you like most to know about the New Testament?

2. As best as you can, make out from this introduction to the study of the New Testament what does it mean "to give voice" to the text of the New Testament?

3. A disciplined approach to the New Testament involves the use of historical method, as well as literary, rhetorical, and theological considerations. Briefly, what is involved in each of these approaches to "giving voice" to the New Testament text?

4. What significance does "testament" have in naming the collection of writings that form the New Testament?

5. Paul Ricoeur distinguishes between three worlds of the text. What are they and how do they apply to the study of the New Testament?

6. Describe the six signs of mature and complete understanding. How do they apply to the study of the New Testament?

Reference Works for the Study of the New Testament:

- *The Catholic Comparative New Testament* (Oxford: Oxford University Press, 2005). Features eight complete translations of the New Testament—all approved for use by Catholics. Comparing the translations gives non-Greek readers a broader sense of the interpretative possibilities.

- *The New Interpreter's Dictionary of the Bible.* 5 volumes. Ed. by Katherine Sakenfeld. Nashville: Abingdon Press, 2006–2010. Contains short, up-to-date articles by scholarly contributors on the writings, themes, characters, places, customs, and other matters related to interpreting the Bible.

- *The New Testament and Its Modern Interpreters.* Ed. by Eldon J. Epp and George W. MacRae. Philadelphia and Atlanta: Fortress Press and Scholars Press, 1989. Surveys the contributions of contemporary scholars to our understanding of the New Testament.

- *Oxford Bible Atlas.* Second Edition. Ed. by Adrian Curtis. London: Oxford University Press, 2009. Contains pictures, articles, maps, and charts detailing many of the geo-political matters related to the study of the New Testament.

- *The Oxford Bible Commentary.* Ed. by John Barton and John Muddiman. Oxford: Oxford University Press, 2001. Contains introductory articles to each of the biblical writings by respected scholars.

Internet Sites for the Study of the New Testament:

- Increasingly students use the internet to conduct research and inform themselves. While there are rich resources out there in cyber space there are also many sites that publish unreliable information on the New Testament. Furthermore, it is difficult to recommend reliable internet sites because unlike print resources internet sites tend to come and go without notice. There are a couple of sites that have proved informative and stable. You might find them helpful as you seek to broaden and deepen your knowledge about the Bible:

  a) Mark Goodacre's site provides information and links to various aspects related to the study of the Bible. It may be accessed at http://ntgateway.com/

  b) David Barr's site also provides information and links to various aspects related to the study of the Bible. It may be accessed at http://www.wright.edu/~david.barr/

c) A good source of background to the historical period era of the New Testament is available from Tufts University. This site may be accessed at http://www.perseus.tufts.edu/

You may locate additional sites via an "advanced Google search," limiting the search to .edu domains.

Chapter **1**

What is the New Testament?

What is the New Testament? What is it good for? Why study it? The questions before us at the outset of our study are important and inter-related. Such questions are answered, at least in part, by the student's horizon of expectation. Students will see in the New Testament only what their horizon of expectation allows them to see. This university course in the study of the New Testament is designed, as university education in other disciplines, to expand expectation and facility so that students may sail beyond the horizon of their home waters into worlds as yet unexplored.

Bible: Book of God

As we anticipate our study of the New Testament the wise counsel of the Shakespeare professor to his students applies. He taught his students that Shakespeare is "vast, colossal, inexhaustible. Shakespeare [is] bigger than any of us, bigger than all of us put together . . . Only by submitting . . . to the plays for months and years on end [will] we ever approach wisdom—by entering their world, by giving ourselves up to their shaping power, by allowing Shakespeare to define our horizons and open our eyes to new realms of understanding."[1] If that is true of Shakespeare, and I absolutely agree that it is, then how much the more is it true of the Bible—Old and New Testaments! Some years ago Gabriel Josipovici, a professor of English, published the report of his encounter with the Bible under the title, *The Book of God: A Response to the Bible.*[2] At the end of his report Josipovici likens the encounter with the Bible to Jacob's encounter with God at the Jabbok (Gen. 32:22–32). "He is now both more and less than he was before the encounter . . . we see him [and ourselves] now within the larger world, created . . . by God."[3] The story of the Bible, the professor of reading concludes, does not leave readers as they were before. Like Jacob, readers too are both less and more. Josipovici has heard the word of the Bible in a way that "brings us more fully to life and makes us want to let others share in the experience."[4] That remains the promise of reading the Bible.

---

[1] Fleming Rutledge, "It's About God," *Princeton Seminary Bulletin*, 23.3 (2002): 345–46.
[2] Gabriel Josipovici, *The Book of God: A Response to the Bible* (New Haven: Yale University Press, 1988).
[3] Ibid., 309.
[4] Ibid.

What is the New Testament About?

At the outset of our course I ask students, "What do you imagine that the New Testament is about?" Their answers are revealing. Many students imagine that the New Testament reports what, according to Jesus, one is to believe and do in order to earn the favor of God and the reward of heaven. No matter which religious tradition they happen to have been reared in—Catholic, Lutheran, Methodist, Baptism, Pentecostal, or none at all—they tend to imagine across the denominational spectrum that the New Testament pictures Jesus as a teacher who instructs people about the religious life, a life of climbing the ladder of good works and right beliefs into heaven. Students are surprised to discover in the actual course of reading the New Testament that its picture of Jesus as teacher is a minor aspect of the portrait. It also surprises students to learn that the New Testament pictures religion moving in the opposite direction, not humans getting up to heaven but God coming down to earth. The New Testament deals less with life in heaven and more with life on earth. The New Testament does not lack a vision of heaven. But it will come as a surprise to most people's expectation how little attention the New Testament, apart from the Book of Revelation, devotes to heaven and its entrance requirements. The New Testament believes with the Old Testament that the human being was created for the down-to-earth life of honoring God as God, enjoying and caring for God's creation in the company of those with whom we share it (see Gen. 2). According to the story of the New Testament, God in Christ comes down to earth to free humans from their anxiety about personal destiny and worth so that they may be free to live out, here and now, their God-given purpose as it takes shape in some earthly **vocation**[5] or another. The New Testament offers very little advice about how one is to live. The central question that occupies the New Testament concerns the freedom to live a truly human life, trusting God as the freely giving God. When the heart trusts God's promise to take care of us as only God can then we are free to be you and me.

Why Study the New Testament?

© 2012 Jupiterimages Corp.

There is wisdom to launching a university education with a course of study in the New Testament, along with other courses that tend the core formation of the human person. The core formation of the person as human begins long before the university years. It began the day each of us was born. Along the way many people have made a contribution to our individual formation as a human being. Not the least of the contributors has been our parents, along with friends, extended family,

---

[5]Vocation refers to the way in which the human being lives out its purpose to enjoy and care for creation. It involves not only one's employment, but as well one's family and community life beyond the work by which one earns a living and contributes to the well being of creation.

teachers and pastors, coaches, and other mentors. Study of the New Testament in the setting of the liberal arts university now seeks to make a further contribution to the humanization of the individual student. The voice of the New Testament when heard in its own voice, the voice of God, says in effect, "I promise to take care of you in this life as well as in the life after this life. Trusting the promise will make you free to concentrate on preparing to serve the well-being of creation. For that I created you." To summarize the way Genesis puts it, the Lord God put the human in the pleasant and good garden of creation to till and keep it (Gen. 2:15).

The encounter with the New Testament promises to enrich our understanding of fundamental religious realities: God, human nature and purpose, faith and freedom, law and grace, and heaven and earth. As one student said of the experience, "The central message of the New Testament turns everything upside down and inside out, including the reader." That student's report of what happens in the course of the encounter with the New Testament writings comes very near to Mark's description of the way in which Jesus sought to prepare people for the encounter with God. Jesus, according to Mark, came into the life of creation like gangbusters, proclaiming the good news of God: "The time is fulfilled, the encounter with God as God is at hand, anchors away, believe the good news, set sail for the adventure of a life time!" (Mark 1:15, my translation).

The encounter with the humanizing "good news" of the New Testament constitutes our primary objective in this course of study. There are however certain realities about the New Testament as a literary artifact of noteworthy importance to the encounter.

What is the New Testament?

There are a number of ways that we can answer the question: What is the New Testament? To this point we have essentially been answering the question on the basis of the message of the New Testament. At the end of the day, the message makes the New Testament worth the bother of reading, studying, pondering, and discussing it. As students will come to appreciate ever more deeply, the message of the New Testament cannot be had apart from the literature of the New Testament. The message of the New Testament emerges out of active engagement with the writings. But the message remains ever entangled with the writings. We will have more to say about this aspect of things in the individual chapters of the study guide. In the remainder of this section we turn our attention to the physicality of the New Testament. What is the New Testament as an artifact from antiquity? There are some things worth knowing, and in fact essential to knowing the truth about the New Testament.

The Impulse to Write it Down

The first Christians belonged to a world that, for a variety of reasons, preferred speaking/hearing over writing/reading. Unlike people today who prefer to have things written down in black and white, the people of antiquity preferred the living voice of oral witness. We have, for example, no evidence that Jesus ever wrote anything down. Furthermore, it appears that for the first twenty years or so, in highly sophisticated fashion, Christians transmitted the message of faith orally. Even after Christians began to commit the testimony of Jesus to written form they continued to value hearing more highly than reading.

Historians offer educated hunches regarding what first moved Christians to document their beliefs and experiences in written form. To some extent the explanation of what moved early Christians to write is more or less readily evident. Paul, for instance, wrote letters as a poor substitute for personal presence. He would have preferred to be physically present to address the cares and affairs of the churches, but circumstances prevented it. Thus, he resorted to writing letters. As he explains to the Thessalonian Christians, "we wanted to come to you . . . again and again—but Satan blocked our way" (1 Thess. 2:18–19). John, the writer of the Apocalypse, explains that he is compelled by divine mandate to put the message of Christ for the churches into written form (Rev. 1:19). Beyond such explanations the impulse that led to committing Christian witness to written form remains a mystery. Perhaps, as some historians suggest, these early Christians were aiming to get down in writing an official version of the Christian truth against **heretical**[6] versions of the Christian message. Or perhaps as time began to stretch out before the Christian movement, community leaders were moved to write down for posterity the witness of faith. At the end of the day, unless archeologists unearth additional evidence, a more complete explanation will continue to remain a mystery. So then, for whatever reason, within twenty years of the death and resurrection of Jesus, Christians began to produce literature of considerable artistic achievement. Eventually some of that literature was collected into what we have before us as the New Testament.

The New Testament as Canon of Christian Scriptures

The writings that comprise the New Testament were written over a period of more or less sixty years, roughly from 50 CE to 110 CE. During this time, Christians produced a considerable volume of literature dedicated to the Christian message. Much of this literature was not to be included in the New Testament. Why only the twenty-seven writings that comprise the New Testament and not the others? The historical story is long and complex. Conspiracy theories abound. This much may be said for sure. The New Testament collection of works was not decided by an authoritarian church intent upon stamping out alternative views which challenged its exclusive hold on the Christian truth. Wherever this view comes from it does not come from the historical evidence. For starters, the New Testament collection was coming into formation well before a church order sufficiently centralized to impose its will on the **canon** of Scripture. The historical evidence points actually in the opposite direction. In a highly decentralized movement believers from diverse geographic regions and realms of experience were finding upon

---

[6]See heresy in Appendix A: Glossary of Terms (p. 122).

20

exposure that some writings were more compelling and helpful than others as they sought to live, understand, and communicate their faith. Familiarity with these writings will lead the student to appreciate their diversity of thought when it comes to understanding the significance of Jesus for faith and life. Within the theological diversity that constitutes the New Testament readers will find themselves caught up in the continuing discussion and debate about what constitutes the heart of faith. Which voices from the New Testament chorus will be heard to carry the melody of the New Testament message for individual readers? The answer cannot be given ahead of time. Once again, the proof of the pudding will be in the tasting. Only reading and giving voice to the various writings will determine what succeeds in claiming the imagination of faith.

Translation and Transmission

Of course before we talk about reading the New Testament and the claims it makes upon us we must think about which version of the New Testament we will read. There is a remarkable variety of English versions available to readers. Just to brush the surface of available editions, there is the King James Version or as it is sometimes known, the Authorized Version of 1611, even though no one, including King James, ever authorized the version (also The Revised King James Version of 1999, The Revised Standard Version of 1955, The New Revised Standard Version of 1989). There are also The New American Edition, the Jerusalem Bible, Today's English Version, the New English Bible, the Douay-Rheims Version, The New American Bible for Catholics, not to mention specialized editions for every imaginable circumstance from nursing mothers to men in military service to transgender people in public life, even a *Reader's Digest* version. How did we get so many versions of the Bible? Is one version better than another? How do they compare to the original? Spending time with such questions will prove worth our attention, particularly as they bear upon the place of the Bible in contemporary life.

Let's begin with the easiest of the questions: How do all these versions compare to the original? The answer is: We do not know. We don't know because we have no original copies of the writings that comprise the New Testament. Rather, what we have are copies of copies. We possess from antiquity about five thousand New Testament manuscripts in varying degrees of completion. Prior to the invention of the printing press in the sixteenth century, texts were transmitted by scribal copyists. Within these manuscripts there are somewhere in the neighborhood of 150,000 instances in which we find different renderings of the same passage. Most of the differences are minor, easily resolved, and insignificant to making out the meaning. A few remain controversial and consequential to our understanding of what has been written. A good annotated study Bible, like The New American Bible for Catholics (TNAB, 1991) or the HarperCollins Study Bible (NRSV, 2003), identifies and comments on such passages. Generally speaking, scholars, across their otherwise diverse differences, are confident that they have reconstructed from the available manuscript evidence the New Testament in its original form and content. Confidence that we have an edition of the New Testament materials that closely resembles the originals runs parallel to our confidence in the work of scholars.

Between contemporary readers and the reconstructed New Testament of the scholars lies one more step in delivering a readable edition. In addition to determining which manuscripts most reliably represent the original writings, someone must prepare a translation of the original Greek into English. Translators face a two-fold challenge in getting from the original Greek of the New Testament to a readable translation for English readers. First, translators must determine how the original Greek would have been read, heard, and understood in its own day. As scholars unearth ever more evidence from the era and as they continue to expand their historical understanding their translations improve in this respect. For example, in the 1955 translation known as the RSV translators modernized thee, thy, and thou. All such pronouns were simply rendered by the English, "you," except when the text was addressing God, in which case thee, thy, and thou were retained. The rationale was that the more formal speech—thee, thy, and thou—expressed special reverence for God. Thus according to this translation the famous Twenty-third Psalm reads, "I fear no evil; for thou art with me; thy rod and thy staff, they comfort me" (v. 4). But by 1995, when the NRSV translation was made, scholars had discovered that the ancients used the same pronouns in addressing God as they used in addressing their neighbors. Thus the 1995 translation of that same verse from Psalm 23 reads: "I fear no evil; for you are with me; your rod and your staff—they comfort me." The NRSV translation more closely approximates how the verse would have sounded in the ears of the ancient audience.

The challenge of translation involves not only determining what the original language meant and how it functioned in the ancient time. As well, translators face the challenge of setting forth the sense of the original into the ever-changing English language of today. Consider for example a passage from Paul's description of ill treatment at the hands of his enemies. In 2 Corinthians he states, "Once I was stoned" (11:25). In 1955 that might have served to explain to readers that Paul had literally been pelted with rocks. But under the cultural and linguistic influence of the 1960s translators thought they had better leave nothing to the imagination and thus the verse was translated, "Once I received a stoning."

Another reality that accounts for the many different versions is that scholars take different approaches to translation. How should the New Testament sound—modern and up-to-date or old fashioned like a Shakespearean classic? Should the translation be a word-for-word literal translation? Or should it strive dynamically to convey the equivalent meaning? No matter which approach translators take to the task they cannot avoid making interpretative decisions. The necessity raises a question: Should the translation avoid theological prejudice? Perhaps an even better question would be: Can translators avoid the influence of theological outlook in the course of translating the Bible? In facing such questions the best translations are produced by scholars who work in teams that are constituted as widely as possible with respect to age, sex, denominational affiliation, theological outlook, as well as fields of competence. Generally, translators devote some attention in the introduction to explaining the approach they have taken to their work. Consider the approach of three popular versions—TEV, NRSV, and TNAB.

The translators of the Good News Bible: The Bible in Today's English Version (TEV, 1976) explain in the preface to their translation that they were aiming "to set forth the Biblical content and message in standard, everyday, natural form of English." Therefore without sacrificing "faithful representation of the cultural and historical features of the original" they sought in their translation to use contemporary language that is natural, clear, simple, and unambiguous."[7] The translators of The New American Bible for Catholics explain that they have "sought to clarify obscure readings and to make the whole more intelligible to contemporary readers."[8] The translators of the New Revised Standard Version provide the most detail about how they approached their work. For the most part they followed the maxim, "As literal as possible, as free as necessary" to render the text appreciably intelligible.

No matter what approach translators have taken interpretative decisions have needed to be made about how best to render the Greek of the original into understandable English. In order to appreciate the interpretative issues involved in making out the sense of the biblical text, contemporary readers are best served by consulting a variety of translations. Consider for example the way in which these three translations render Paul's famous summary statement of the Christian good news in Romans 1:16–17.

TEV: "I have complete confidence in the gospel; it is God's power to save all who believe, first the Jews and also the Gentiles. For the gospel reveals how God puts people right with himself: it is through faith from beginning to end. As the scripture says, 'The person who is put right with God through faith shall live.'"

NRSV: "For I am not ashamed of the gospel; it is the power of God for salvation to everyone who has faith, to the Jew first and also to the Greek. For in it the righteousness of God is revealed through faith for faith; as it is written, 'The one who is righteous will live by faith.'"

TNAB: "For I am not ashamed of the gospel. It is the power of God for the salvation of everyone who believes: for the Jew first, and then Greek. For in it is revealed the righteousness of God from faith to faith; as it is written, 'The one who is righteous by faith will live.'"

Putting these translations side by side reveals a couple of interesting things. In the first place, it is evident that the TNAB and the NRSV have taken a literal, word-for-word approach to rendering the Greek into English. Both translations render Paul's opening statement in exactly the same wording: "For I am not ashamed of the gospel." But the meaning of the opening can be taken differently, as the respective note in each edition explains. The TNAB explains, "Paul is not ashamed to proclaim the gospel, despite the criticism." The NRSV however explains that the phrase is "probably a stylistic understatement meaning, "I am proud of." The TEV agrees with the NRSV and has sought to

---

[7] *Good News Bible: Today's English Version* (New York: American Bible Society, 1976) Preface, no page numbers.
[8] *The New American Bible for Catholics* (Nashville: Thomas Nelson Publishers, 1969), x.

translate Paul's sense accordingly: "I have complete confidence in the gospel; it is God's power to save . . ." (Rom. 1:16).

Likewise the concluding statement of Paul's summary statement is subject to interpretation. The range of possibilities is expressed in the translations:

TEV: "The one who is put right by God through faith will live."

NAB: "The one who is righteous by faith will live."

NRSV: "The one who is righteous will live by faith."

So, does one become righteous by faith or by God through faith? Or is living by faith a sign of one's righteousness? How such interpretative issues are to be resolved is complex and will be addressed in the chapters that follow. The point for the moment is that students of the New Testament will be made aware of the interpretative issues by comparing a variety of translations.

The Bible: Library of God's Word

© 2012 JupiterImages Corp.

Now that we have some insight into the process of making the Bible, an artifact from antiquity, available to a contemporary audience, we are ready to take a look inside to see what the Bible contains. With respect to its contents the Bible is well named. Bible means a library of books. And that is exactly what we have in the Bible, a collection of writings by various authors, most of them anonymous, written over many centuries.

In the little library of the Bible there are two main divisions. The division in the first part of the Bible is shared by Jews and Christians as Scripture. It is stylish among scholars to refer to these books as the Hebrew Bible. This name is derived from the fact that most of the writings are originally written in the Hebrew language. Scholars prefer the terminology because it references the writings without prejudice of a particular theological understanding. However, the reality is that, both historically and contemporaneously, Jews and Christians do read, or interpret, these writings differently. Scholarly treatment of the Bible would be better served by respecting the integrity of Jewish and Christian regard for their respective Scriptures.

The first century, the time when the writings that eventually form the New Testament were written, saw the emergence of "two Judaisms." As Robert Jenson, a Christian theologian, explains,

. . . after the catastrophe of the Jewish wars with Rome [66–70 CE] and the destruction of the Temple [70 CE] two Judaisms survived: the then emerging church of Jews and gentiles and the Judaism created by

© 2012 JupiterImages Corp.

the rabbis of Mishnah and Talmud . . . Each has its defining way of reading Israel's Scripture: the church reads it as narrative leading to Christ and the Kingdom; the rabbinic synagogue reads it as timeless *torah*. Strictly historically, neither community of interpretation has a prior justification or claim . . . nor therefore is either mode of interpretation more literal or straightforward than the other.[9]

Alan Segal, a Jewish historian, agrees with Jenson's view. He writes,

It is a startling truth that the religions we know today as Judaism and Christianity were born at the same time and nurtured in the same environment . . . they followed different paths . . . Like Rebecca's children, Judaism and Christianity had a history of conflict. But like them, they may reach a reconciliation based upon mutual understanding and respect.[10]

© 2012 JupiterImages Corp.

Today Jews and Christians do seek to cultivate mutual respect and understanding. The issues which establish the agenda for the dialogue between Christians and Jews on the question of Scripture are complex, deep, and sensitive. It will not proceed constructively apart from listening and speaking to one another with respect to how each community reads and understands its Scriptures.[11]

In the worshiping community of Judaism, Jews speak of their scriptural writings as TANAKH. Tanakh is a transliteration of a Hebrew acronym which stands for the Books of the Law (Torah), the Writings (K'tuvim), and the Prophets (Nevi'im), the writings which comprise the Jewish Scriptures. Christians refer to these same writings as the Old Testament. Donald Juel has pointed out that at the time when the New Testament writings were composed the designations, Old and New Testament, were not in use. Furthermore, Christians read the Jewish Scriptures (Old Testament) in Greek, the so-called Septuagint. Therefore it might be more accurate to speak of the Old Testament as Israel's Scriptures. However we name the divisions of the Bible, the critical thing is to treat them in a way that respects their status in the Christian community and in the Jewish community as Scripture.

The Jewish community reads Tanakh through the lens of the Mishnah as "timeless *torah.*" Christians read the Old Testament through the lens of the New Testament. That is, Christians believe that by his death and resurrection Jesus is vindicated as the Messiah of Israel. This conviction of faith lies at the heart of the New Testament proclamation. Robert Jenson sees this reality as the touch stone in the church's relation to Judaism.

---

[9]Robert Jenson, "The Religious Power of Scripture," *Scottish Journal of Theology,* 52.1 (1999): 104.

[10]Alan Segal, *Rebecca's Children: Judaism and Christianity in the Roman World* (Cambridge: Harvard University Press, 1986), 1, 12.

[11]See for further discussion of the question the excellent article by the Jewish scholar, Jon D. Leveanson, "How Not to Conduct Jewish-Christian Dialogue," *Commentary,* December (2001): 31–37. The volume, *Rebecca's Children,* by Alan Siegel, offers a helpful way to view the differences between Judaism and Christianity with respect to current inter-religious dialogue and the origins of the two faiths.

If the church's faith is true, Christ is the incarnate torah; so that the claim overlaps that of the synagogue without cancelling it. Therefore the church has no reason either to defer to rabbinic exegesis or to regard it as irrelevant or a priori false. What judgment the synagogue should make of the church's **exegesis** is of course not to be prompted by the church.[12]

Inside the New Testament

The collection of the New Testament literature divides into three sections: narratives (5), letters (21), and apocalypse (1). In the chapter on literary analysis we discuss the characteristics of each of these genres and an approach to respectful and fruitful engagement with them. Here we may briefly describe the character and content of each of the twenty-seven writings.

We may begin with the letters. There are essentially two groups of letters in the New Testament: 1) the letters under the influence of the Apostle Paul and 2) the general **epistles**.[13] In chapter two we briefly describe each of the letters. Thirteen of the twenty-seven writings that comprise the New Testament bear the name of Paul. These thirteen can be divided into three groups: A) Seven Undisputed Letters of Paul. Scholars are generally agreed that Paul without doubt wrote these letters. B) Three Deutero-Letters of Paul. While these letters bear the name of Paul as author, scholarly opinion is divided over the question whether Paul actually wrote them. The majority opinion is that these letters were written either by a student or colleague of Paul after his death to represent his point of view on some unprecedented question. C) The final group of letters that bear the name of Paul address the question of church leadership. For a variety of reasons scholars are of the opinion that while Paul most likely did not write the so-called Pastoral Letters in some measure they bear the influence of his theological outlook on the question of church leadership.

Undisputed Letters of Paul	Deutero-Letters of Paul	Pastoral Epistles
1 Thessalonians	2 Thessalonians	1 Timothy
1 Corinthians	Ephesians	2 Timothy
2 Corinthians	Colossians	Titus
Galatians		
Philippians		
Philemon		
Romans		

---

[12] Jenson, "The Religious Power of Scripture," 105.
[13] Epistle is another term for letter.

Of the 449 pages that comprise the New Testament in the Harper Collins Study edition of the Bible, 123 pages are devoted to writings under the influence of Paul. The only other writer who comes close to as much space in the New Testament is Luke, and three fourths of his story of the church is devoted to the career of Paul. Why does the New Testament devote so much attention to Paul?

Two things explain Paul's popularity among early Christians. In the first place, more than the efforts of any other person in antiquity Paul's work on behalf of the gospel expands the borders of the Christian movement far and wide. Over the course of his career he established churches all throughout the Mediterranean region. Moreover, Paul may be regarded as the first and most compelling, if also controversial, theologian of the Christian movement.

Seven Undisputed Letters of Paul

The earliest writings of the New Testament are the seven undisputed Letters of Paul. Beyond the consensus that the letters were written during the decade of the 50s, there is little scholarly agreement regarding exactly where and when. Each letter bears the name of the recipient community. Written for the most part to Christian congregations which he had established, they address issues which have arisen in the course of the membership's life together in the larger socio-political world of the Greco-Roman era. These letters provide a wealth of information regarding the conditions and struggles of the early Christian communities as they sought to make their way in faith. As well, the letters set forth the way in which the Christian message was understood in the Pauline communities of the faith. In the chapter on literary analysis we will have more to say about the challenge of reading these letters. Here we briefly describe the character and content of the letters. The current canonical order, preserved here in the presentation of the letters, seems to reflect an early collection of Paul's letters arranged according to length, longest to shortest.

Romans is one of two exceptions to the general rule that the undisputed letters were written to congregations Paul had himself established. It appears that Paul has written the letter to the Roman congregation to introduce himself and his message in the interest of soliciting the congregation's support for the planned expansion of his missionary efforts into the west (15:1–33). Witten in the standard Greco-Roman form, the body of the letter divides into two parts: the theological argument (1:16–11:36) and the exhortations (12:1–15:58). The theme of the letter (1:16–17) sets forth Paul's understanding of the Christian gospel. Accordingly Paul contends that the death and resurrection of Jesus reveals God's saving righteousness enacted as God's justification of the ungodly (3:9–26). The theme is developed in terms of Christian self-understanding (chapters 3–8) and in terms of God's commitment to Israel (chapters 9–11). In the second part of the letter's main section Paul develops the implication of the gospel for the way in which Christians live together and in relation to their non-Christian neighbors (chapters 12–15). In both sections, as Leander Keck points out in his introduction to the letter, Paul proves himself a master of Greco-Roman rhetorical techniques and Jewish exegetical methods.[14]

First Corinthians was likely written in 54 CE to the troubled congregation in Corinth. The congregation had been established by Paul several years before the letter was written. In the meantime the congregation has hosted a number of other apostolic leaders over whose leadership the membership has become divided (1:10–12). The letter is written in two parts. In the chapters 1–6 Paul addresses the divisions and in chapters 7–16 he addresses controversial issues which have arisen in the course of the congregation's life together. Paul seeks to counsel the congregation from the perspective of Christian message (1:26–31; 6:9–11; 12:12–13). In the course of offering his counsel Paul demonstrates his diplomatic and rhetorical facility as taught and practiced by the Greek teachers of the time.

Second Corinthians, probably written a year or so after the earlier letter, provides evidence that the controversies troubling the congregation continued unabated. In fact the first letter may have made matters worse (2:2–3). The perceived disjointedness of the letter has led to many theories about its composition. Nonetheless contemporary readers find in the letter much theological food for thought regarding what it means to live by faith in difficult circumstances (4:16–5:10), the nature of Christian mission (3:1–18), the nature of forgiveness and reconciliation (2:5–11; 5:11–6:11), and much more.

Galatians, the most polemical of Paul's letters, is difficult to date. While some scholars are inclined to date it as early as 48–49 CE, most scholars prefer a date in the latter half of the decade of the 50s. In the letter Paul defends his ministry and message to the Galatian Christians. Expressing astonishment and dismay over the fact that the Galatians have embraced a gospel contrary to what he had proclaimed (1:6–9), Paul seeks to restore their faith in the gospel of God's justification of the ungodly apart from works of the law (2:15–5:26).

Philippians was written during one of Paul's many imprisonments (1:7), which provides the occasion of the letter. Paul writes in part to express his gratitude for the unwavering support of the Philippian Christians, including their help during his current imprisonment (2:25; 4:10–20). While he acknowledges that both he and the Philippians may have reason for disappointment and concern, nonetheless, they share mutual joy over the way in which God uses all circumstances to advance the spread of the gospel (1:10b–26). As well, no matter what circumstance Christians may find themselves in, it may serve as the occasion to live as "little Christs" to the neighbor (2:5–11).

First Thessalonians is the earliest of Paul's Letters, probably written from Corinth around 50 CE. It appears to have been occasioned by the report of Paul's co-worker Timothy who at Paul's request had recently made a visit to the congregation (3:6–10). In the letter Paul encourages the Thessalonians in their mutual care for and building up of

---

[14]See *The Harper Collins Study Bible, Revised Edition*, ed. by Wayne Meeks (San Francisco: Harper Collins Publishers, 2006), 1910.

one another in faith (5:11). Readers of the letter cannot fail to be impressed by the affectionate and encouraging tone of the letter. At one point Paul compares himself to a "nurse tenderly caring for her own children" (2:7). He refers to the Thessalonian Christians as "his glory and joy" (2:20).

Philemon was probably written from the mid to the late 50s while Paul was in prison, though exactly where is difficult to determine. The short letter is addressed to Philemon, a prominent member of a Pauline congregation. Paul is writing on behalf of a slave, Onesimus, who has been "separated from" his master Philemon. During his run-away flight Onesimus had apparently been converted to the Christian faith under Paul's care. In a masterfully diplomatic way Paul encourages Philemon to accept the returning Onesimus "as you would welcome me . . . a beloved brother" (v. 17, 16). In fact the letter is so diplomatically successful that it is difficult to determine exactly what action Paul intended Philemon to take.

The Three Deutero-Pauline Letters

These three New Testament letters—2 Thessalonians, Ephesians, and Colossians—in the majority opinion of scholars, were most likely written by students or colleagues of Paul following his death to represent his point of view in circumstances that were unprecedented during his lifetime. The judgment is based primarily on consideration of subject matter, style, vocabulary, and theological outlook. The date and place of composition is difficult to pinpoint beyond the view that they are written during the last third of the first century.

Ephesians unfolds as a comprehensive treatise on the Christian life of faith, hope, and love. The letter addresses Gentiles "who were once far off . . . without God" but who have now "been brought near by the blood of Christ" (2:12–13). The author of the letter encourages these new believers to renounce their former ways (5:3–20) and live a "life worthy of their calling" (4:1). The letter brings out the implication of living by faith in God's promise of salvation and by love for the neighbor, especially as the neighbor is encountered in the other members of the household (5:21–6:9). The final exhortation (6:10–20) reminds its hearers that the struggle of faith is against the "spiritual forces of evil" (6:12) therefore they ought to "take up the full armor of God" (6:13).

Colossians is best read as a brief sermon on the adequacy of the baptismal promise to sustain Christians in the life of faith (2:11–12). Trusting God to keep God's promise Christians are free to serve the neighbor in whatever circumstance they find themselves. As God's chosen people Christian are to clothe themselves "with compassion, kindness, humility, meekness, and patience . . . above all with love, which binds everything together in perfect harmony" (3:12–14).

Second Thessalonians seeks to assure the Christians in Thessalonica of Christ's promised return to "give relief to the afflicted . . . inflicting vengeance on those who do not know God and on those who do not obey the gospel" (1:5–8).

Pastoral Epistles

Though these three letters—First and Second Timothy and Titus—bear the name of Paul, scholars are persuaded that Paul did not write them. They are similar in style, vocabulary, and theological outlook to one another, but in all of those ways dissimilar to the undisputed letters of Paul. Admittedly one may hear echoes of Paul's theology in the letters, but these echoes are developed in more Hellenistic forms of expression with the question of church leadership in mind. The letters presume a church order more formally and hierarchically developed than in the churches during the lifetime of Paul (50s). These letters also evidence echoes of the Imperial Cult and for that reason scholars date them during the Flavian Dynasty (69–96 CE), or perhaps during the reign of Trajan (98–117 CE). By this time Paul's co-workers, Timothy and Titus, would have been dead, thus here in the Pastoral Epistles the names function symbolically to name ideal church leaders.

First Timothy warns against the danger of false teachers who "occupy themselves with myths . . . that promote speculation" (1:4). Instead, true teachers of the faith center their preaching on the merciful determination of God revealed in Jesus to save sinners (1:12–16; 6:3–10). Accordingly Christians may be instructed in the life of prayer (2:1–15), providing for the well-being of the fellowship (5:1–6:2), and fighting the good fight of faith (6:11–19). The remainder of the letter sets forth the qualifications for positions of church leadership (3:1–4:16).

Second Timothy. Unlike 1 Timothy, which focuses on the order and office of church leadership, 2 Timothy offers personal encouragement to a younger colleague "suffering for the gospel" (1:8): "always be sober, endure suffering, do the work of an evangelist, carry out your ministry fully" (4:5).

Titus is addressed to Paul's co-worker by that name. The letter instructs Titus with respect to his ministry among the Christians of Crete where he has been "left behind" to find, train, and appoint local leaders (1:5–9). Tucked into the advice is the promise of God to believers in their baptism (3:4–8). The promise establishes the solid foundation upon which the community of faith has its life.

General Epistles

For our purposes we may consider the remaining eight letters of the New Testament under the rubric of the general epistles.

Hebrews, according to scholarly convention, was penned anonymously in the last third of the first century. Although the piece ends like a letter (13:22–25), in the main it reads more like a sermon. The geographic location of the congregation for which the sermon was intended is difficult to make out. Some scholars reason on the basis of the closing salutation and other external evidence that the congregation might have been located in Rome. What is more certain from the letter itself is that the congregation, no matter where it was located, is comprised of second generation Christians (2:3). Under the pressure of persecution members of the congregation are in danger of "drifting away" from the faith and in fact some may already have renounced the faith and returned to their former ways and beliefs (2:1; 6:1–12). Against this prospect the author encourages the members of the congregation to remain faithful because their great high priest, Jesus Christ, remains faithful to them and has withheld nothing, including his own life, to include and sustain them among his own people (see especially chapter 10).

James is included in the New Testament, but with reservation by significant theologians, not the least of whom is the sixteenth-century reformer, Martin Luther. Luther held the work in small esteem because it contradicts Paul's contention that believers are saved or justified by faith in the promise of Jesus. In the time of Luther as well as today other theologians contend against such reservations that James offers a necessary corrective to Paul, namely, that faith without works is dead (2:14–26). In that spirit, James admonishes the community to "be doers of the word, and not merely hearers" (1:19).

First Peter, according to the opening salutation, is sent to Christians scattered throughout provinces of the Roman Empire in Asia Minor (1:1–2). These Christians are living in deep tension with their non-Christian neighbors. Because of their public refusal to go along with the sanctioned religion of the Roman Empire, Christians were misunderstood, ostracized, ridiculed, and at times physically persecuted for their conviction that Jesus alone deserves to be honored and worshiped as God. Their situation might have seemed a contradiction of the baptismal promise, but as the letter reassures these believers, their suffering binds them in solidarity with the Lord (2:18–25; 4:1–19).

Second Peter is patterned after the literary form of a "testament." Accordingly, it sets forth the testimony of faith for which the Apostle Peter wants to be remembered in death (1:12–15). While not contesting its literary form most scholars contend, primarily on the basis of 3:3–4, that it was written not by Peter, but by an anonymous Christian who lived in the second generation of believers. The letter/testament addresses the crisis by the perceived delay in Christ's second coming: "scoffers will come . . . saying, 'Where is the promise of his coming? For ever since our ancestors died, all things continue as they were from the beginning of creation!'" (3:4). Against the false conclusion, 2 Peter offers assurance that those who put their faith and hope in God's promise of a new heaven and a new earth will not be disappointed (3:8–13).

First John, though commonly referred to as a letter, lacks the customary opening and closing salutation of a Greco-Roman letter. According to the actual form of the piece it appears more like a sermon which encourages Christians to "love one another as Christ has loved them" (3:11–24). Echoing the language of the Fourth Gospel the letter contends that to live in selfless love for the neighbor by faith is to walk in the light of God who is love incarnate (4:7–21).

Second John has all the marks of an actual letter. It is addressed to the congregation of believers, symbolized as the "elect lady and her children" (1:1). The author identifies himself as the elder (1:1), who assumes responsibility for the well-being of the congregation. He assures the congregation that to walk in truth and to walk in love are one in the same way of living (vv. 4–6).

Third John is, like 2 John, a letter authored by the elder and addressed to "the beloved Gaius" (v.1), who is commended for "walking in truth" (v. 2) and for extending hospitality to the stranger as though a long lost friend (vv. 5–8).

Jude opposes those who take Christian freedom as license to do whatever pleases the self (vv. 3–4). Against such a false understanding of freedom the letter confirms that true freedom is the freedom to serve the well being of the neighbor in faith (vv. 17–23).

Apocalypse

There is no getting around the fact that the last "book" of the New Testament is by far the strangest writing of them all. Revelation is unlike the rest of the New Testament literature in a number of respects. Like the book of James, Revelation too is included in the New Testament with reservation. Historically, readers of Revelation have been disturbed by the way in which it depicts enemies of faith as monsters and beasts that will be destroyed in the lake of fire. There is no question that monster stories can be dangerous. But they can also be illuminating. Part of the human fascination with monster stories— like the *Terminator, Lord of the Ring, Star Wars, The Lion King, Frankenstein*—is that such stories treat in mythical fashion the danger by which humans overstep their creaturely bounds and begin to lord it over others. Sadly, history provides plenty of evidence to confirm the ever-present danger.

Revelation can be understood on two levels. At one level Revelation offers a theological interpretation of history, specifically the history in which Christians of the Roman Empire find themselves in the last decade of the first century. It was a perilous time for Christians. At this time the public life of the empire revolved around the worship of the emperor as God. Christians in obedience to the First Commandment of their faith were not at liberty to make this concession. Their neighbors were not the least bit understanding. They applied pressure—economic, political, and social—to compel Christians to "go along to get along" with the party line of the state. Christians never knew when the ostracism, discrimination, and ridicule might explode into violence against them. For this reason some Christians were tempted to compromise their faith in public. John writes to seven churches under his pastoral care. In the strongest terms he voices his opposition to the adoption of such a strategy. He warns that God is the beginning and the ending of history (1:8; 22:13) and that the enemies of God along with Christians who compromise their faith in public will be cast into the lake of fire (19:20–21). True Christians will not lose heart but will remain true, both in private and in public, to the gospel. History, no matter what outward events may suggest to the contrary, will find its culmination in the saving promise of God.

At another level Revelation may be understood as a theological interpretation of human experience. At this level the same question provides the drama of the play. The destiny of humans depends upon who they have as God. Apart from the true God we are bound to take playing God for ourselves and others. The only salvation from such a monstrous prospect is when the true God comes and fills that place for us. The proclamation of Revelation in that sense sounds much like the proclamation of Christian baptism where the Lord God declares, "I am the Lord your God. You need no others. I alone can carry the freight of providing for you that you may be free to live a down-to-earth life of enjoying and caring for creation along with the neighbors with whom you are given to share it."

Gospel Narratives and the Acts of the Apostles

The third type of material that readers encounter in the New Testament unfolds as narrative. Five works may be so classified—the four Gospels and the Acts of the Apostles. The Gospels tell the story of Jesus. Acts of the Apostles tells the story of the formation and expansion of the church. Three of the Gospels are very similar to one another—Matthew, Mark, and Luke. In broad outline the story of Jesus develops along the same lines. His public career lasts less than a year. It begins in Galilee and extends to the last week of his life which transpires in Jerusalem. Many of the reports of his doings and sayings are to be found in all three versions of the story. These Gospels have been tagged the synoptic Gospels. Synoptic means to view together and refers to the scholarly habit of studying these writings side by side. However, the more one studies these three stories of Jesus side by side the more you come to appreciate their differences. They all share the conviction that Jesus deserves to be worshipped as the crucified and risen Messiah of God. But in the course of bringing out the significance of this truth for the life of faith they each take a somewhat different approach. The individual descriptions, below, will bear this out.

Narratives of the New Testament			
Synoptic Gospels			
The Gospel According to St. Matthew (composed in 80s)	The Gospel According to St. Mark (composed around 70)	The Gospel According to St. Luke and The Acts of the Apostles (composed in 90s)	The Gospel According to St. John (composed in 90s)
Similar to one another • Public career of Jesus lasts one year • Makes one trip to Jerusalem • Teaches in Parables • Miracles are central to the ministry of Jesus • Casts out demons • Crucified and Risen Messiah of Israel			Different from the synoptic tradition • Public career of Jesus lasts three years • Travels back and forth between Jerusalem and Galilee • Extended conversations; "I am" sayings central to the portrait of Jesus = Speech of God come down • Much symbolism: light/darkness; water; wine; bread; fish; etc. • Book of Signs

John's Gospel clearly belongs to another time and place than the synoptic Gospels. There are marked differences between John and the synoptic Gospels. For example, whereas in the synoptic tradition Jesus makes one fateful trip to Jerusalem at the end of his life, according to John Jesus makes repeated trips back and forth between Jerusalem and Galilee in the course of his life. Whereas the public career of Jesus lasts a year or less in the synoptic tradition, in John's Gospel it lasts at least three years. The two traditions—synoptic and Johannine—portray Jesus differently.

Finally, we come to the Acts of the Apostles. This work though separated in the canonical order by the Gospel of John, was actually written by the same author who wrote the Gospel According to Luke. This writer was as far as we know the first author to connect the story of Jesus to the story of the church. The fact that twenty centuries later we still take this connection for granted only attests the remarkable achievement of this remarkable author.

The Gospel According to St. Mark. For a variety of reasons historians generally take the view that Mark was the first to write the story of Jesus. If we take verse one as the title[15] of his piece then it seems apparent that Mark's purpose was to tell the story of Jesus in such a way as to bring out the significance for faith: "The beginning of the good news of Jesus, the Christ, Son of God." The Greek term, translated here as good news, is the word that Paul had adopted to reference the message of the Christian faith. In English script the Greek word can be transliterated[16] as *euangelion*. An *euangelion* is literally a report of good news. Mark now adopts the word to describe the kind of narrative he seeks to write about Jesus. It is a narrative that tells not only what Jesus said and did but serves by the way the story is told to bring out the good news of Jesus for faith. In order to get the message of Mark, as well as the other Gospel stories of Jesus, it is as important to pay attention not only to what is told about Jesus but how it is told. This is an aspect of things that we will discuss in greater detail in chapter three. For now we may note in brief the character and content of Mark's Gospel.

Accordingly, Mark portrays Jesus as a man of action. Throughout the story the word of Jesus impresses people with its capacity to bring about that of which it speaks. Like the word of God in the story of Genesis 1 the word of Jesus has power to create new realities. God said "let there be" and the creation came into being. In the same way the word of Jesus calls forth a new reality. In his first public act, for example, he meets a man who is possessed of a demon. With the flick of a word Jesus liberates the man from the demon. The people who witness the act of Jesus declare, "What is this? A new teaching—with authority! He commands even the unclean spirits, and they obey him" (1:27b). In the course of the story Jesus proves to be a man/God of his word. In contrast

---

[15]The exact origin of the ascriptions, "The Gospel According to . . . ," remains uncertain, but these designations were in use by the middle of the second century.

[16]Transliteration is a means by which the sound of a word in the original language is represented in the recipient language.

to the human characters in the story who prove to be unfaithful to their promises to Jesus, Jesus keeps his promises even when people misunderstand, betray, deny, ridicule, and finally kill him. Not even death can prevent him from keeping his promises. For this reason God raises him up, alive, to keep his promises, the most important of which will prove to be the one which he makes in chapter two: "those who are well have no need of a physician, but those who are sick; I have come to call not the righteous but sinners" (2:17). Apart from Jesus keeping that promise there would be no good news for Mark to tell.

The Gospel According to St. Matthew divides into five sections, perhaps patterned after the five books of Moses in the Old Testament. In the theological imagination of Israel Moses was viewed as the teacher of faith par excellence. Exactly in that way Matthew portrays Jesus, as a teacher, greater than Moses. To be sure, Matthew portrays Jesus as Messiah as well as teacher, but the emphasis of the story is on Jesus as teacher of the higher righteousness (5:20). In keeping with the theme Matthew anchors the story around five sermons of Jesus—Sermon on the Mount (5–7), On the Mission of Faith (10), Parables of the Kingdom (13), Sermon on Life Together (18), and the Sermon on the Last Judgment (25).

The Gospel According to St. Luke and the Acts of the Apostles. The author of the third Gospel and the Acts of the Apostles proves himself by far the most ambitious and accomplished storyteller in the New Testament. He is the first writer to connect the story of Jesus to the story of the church. As he makes clear in one of the most carefully and elegantly crafted passages in all the Scriptures (Luke 1:1–4), he tells the story of Jesus to demonstrate for his audience "the truth concerning the things about which you have been instructed" (1:4). And the truth, as the angels declare to the shepherds, is that Jesus comes into the world as "good news of great joy for all the people; to you is born this day in the city of David a Savior, who is the Messiah, the Lord" (2:10b–11). However, as the prophet Simeon explains to Mary, "This child is destined for the falling and the rising of many in Israel, and to be a sign that will be opposed so that the inner thoughts of many will be revealed" (2:34–35a). Ironically, it is the people who imagined that they knew Jesus best, for example, his neighbors in his home town and the Temple leaders who reject Jesus. The enemies of Jesus do not undertake their opposition lightly. After his inaugural sermon the people of Nazareth, his hometown, are so enraged against Jesus that they want to pitch him off the highest and nearest hill (4:16–30). And from the very first encounter with him the Temple leaders plot the death of Jesus (22:1–2). In the end, against the judgment of his adversaries, God, by raising the crucified Jesus to new life, vindicates him as true Messiah.

Jesus entrusts the gospel truth to his disciples who bear it to all the world, beginning from Jerusalem (Luke 24:44–49). The Holy Spirit of God empowers them for their mission (Acts 2:1–30). From that Pentecost moment in Jerusalem the spread of the good news about Jesus proves unstoppable. Despite continuing opposition and adversity the good news of Jesus succeeds in reaching the ends of the earth and in turning the world upside down.

Luke's story of those early days of the church is not to be missed. As Jaroslav Pelikan has summarized it:

> Acts is a book of frenetic action . . . Conspiracy, intrigue and ambush, hostile confrontations and fierce conflicts sometimes to the death, rioting, lynch mobs and personal violence . . . incessant travel on an Odysseus-like scale all over the Mediterranean world, complete with shipwreck and venomous serpents, "chains and imprisonment" . . . followed in at least two instances by a successful jailbreak, though only with the aid of celestial mechanics . . . famine and earthquake, crime and punishment, sometimes even without any crime ever having been committed . . . And more touches of humor than all the other books of the New Testament combined.[17]

The Gospel According to St. John in many ways plays very different than the synoptic Gospels. But for all its differences, in the most important respect John demonstrates complete solidarity with the other writers of the New Testament. He believes that Jesus lives and speaks as the decisive word on the question of God. In fact John understands Jesus as very word of God, come down, embodied as a human being, to give life and to make God known (1:1–18; see also 14:8–14). Thus the encounter with Jesus determines one's fate with God (12:44–50). This then constitutes John's purpose in telling the story of Jesus. As he puts it, "Jesus did many other signs in the presence of his disciples, which are not written in this book. But these are written so that you may come to believe that Jesus is the Messiah, the Son of God, and that through believing you may have life in his name" (20:30–31).

Ironically, according to John's story, not everyone has ears for the word of God as spoken by Jesus. Jesus, as God, receives a mixed reception. John, in the prologue, anticipates exactly this turn of events: "He was in the world, and the world came into being through him; yet the world did not know him. He came to what was his own, and his own people did not accept him. But to all who received him, who believed in his name, he gave power to become children of God, who were born, not of blood or of the will of the flesh or of the will of man, but of God" (1:10–13). In part John explains the controversy by the ironic fact that in order to speak to humanity God made himself human (1:18; 3:31–36; 5:19–29). Unfortunately, that's all that some people could see, a human being merely masquerading as God, but not God at all (10:31–39). The controversy of Jesus is not just the failure to see the works of God in Jesus. People could not bring themselves to believe that Jesus speaks for God (5:18; 6:41–71; 8:39–59; 10:22–31). In the end the controversy of Jesus swirls around the question of human freedom. As Jesus explains to the narrative characters in chapter eight, he has come into the world to make people free (8:31–32). The people however deny that they are, or ever had been, enslaved to anyone (8:33–38). Jesus counters that those who commit sin are slave to sin (8:34–35) and thus are at the mercy of God's liberating word (8:36). This then speaks to the promise of Jesus. Literally he is the life of humanity (1:1–5) as all of the "I AM" passages make clear.

---

[17] *Acts.* Brazos Theological Commentary on the Bible (Grand Rapids: Brazos Press, 2005), 23.

Jesus declares that he is all things necessary to life: "I am the Bread of Life, Living Water, grace and truth, the good Shepherd, the Vine, Light of the world." And he comes to pour himself out to give life and the freedom to live it. John's Gospel could not be better summed up than he himself articulates the message of Jesus in what is perhaps the most famous verse of the entire Bible: "For God so loved the world that he gave his only son, so that everyone who believes in him may not perish but may have eternal life" (3:16). The verse not only sums up the message of John's Gospel but the message of the entire Christian Bible.

Terms:

Vocation	Septuagint
Heresy	Exegesis
Canon	Epistle
Bible	Gospel (as a literary designation);
Old Testament	gospel (as a designation of the
New Testament	Christian message)
Tanakh	Synoptic
Israel's Scriptures	Apocalypse

Study Questions:

1. What do you imagine the New Testament is about?

2. What do you perceive to be at stake in the way in which we designate the divisions of the Christian Bible? In what sense are such terms as Hebrew Bible, Septuagint, Israel's Scriptures, Old Testament, New Testament appropriate and inappropriate?

3. What is the original language of the New Testament writings? What is the original language of Israel's Scriptures? In what language did the writers of the New Testament read the Scriptures of Israel? What issues do translators face in rendering the New Testament materials into the English of today?

4. Name the literary divisions of the New Testament.

5. Name and briefly describe the authentic letters of Paul, the Deutero-Pauline letters and the Pastoral Epistles.

6. Briefly characterize the differences and similarities in which the four Gospels tell the story of Jesus.

Recommended Reading

Brevard S. Childs. *The New Testament as Canon: An Introduction.* Philadelphia: Fortress Press, 1984. Argues that the individual works that comprise the New Testament must be interpreted in relation to one another in order to see them as Christian Scripture.

Gamble, Harry. *The New Testament Canon: Its Making and Meaning.* Philadelphia: Fortress Press, 1985. Explains the historical and theological forces that shaped the New Testament canon as Scripture of the Christian church.

Lewis, Jack P. *The English Bible from KJV to NIV: A History and Evaluation.* Grand Rapids: Baker Book House, 1982. Review of translations from the 17th century to modern times.

Parker, D. C. *An Introduction to the New Testament Manuscripts and Their Texts.* Cambridge: Cambridge University Press, 2008. Describes the New Testament manuscripts and other related ancient textual evidence, and the tools needed to study them.

Wegner, Paul D. *The Journey from Texts to Translations: The Origin and Development of the Bible.* Grand Rapids: Baker Book House, 2000. Review of many translations and the history of their production.

Chapter **2**

What is Theology?

This chapter presents a working definition of theology and briefly surveys the formative contribution of the Greeks, along with the contribution of three historic and influential Christian theologians—Augustine of Hippo, Martin Luther, and Ignatius of Loyola. The aim of the chapter is to expand our collegial[1] understanding of what it means to enter into theological discourse in the course of reading the New Testament.

The word "**theology**" consists of two Greek roots—"logy" (logos = language) and "theo" (theos = God). Thus, whenever we are reading, talking, or writing about God and human life in relation to God we have entered upon the subject matter of theology. On the basis of what we have said in the earlier chapters it should more or less be evident that the New Testament from beginning to end qualifies as the subject matter of theology. When we enter upon discussion of the New Testament we have entered into theological discussion. In fact the New Testament, along with the Old Testament, provides, according to the Christian church, the foundational basis for theological reflection on the question of God and human life. Theologians who have learned to hear the Bible in its own voice suffer a radical reversal in their thinking about theological existence. From almost the beginning of time, according to the Bible, humans seem automatically to assume that the goal of life is to climb the ladder of good works and right beliefs to the heights of religious and moral perfection, qualifying for admittance to heaven, or whatever aspiration people like to imagine as the goal of life. Such "ladder theologians" generally assume that humans, prone to missteps and back-sliding, may not be capable of climbing the ladder unassisted, but if they do their best Jesus will "graciously" provide the necessary boost to get them over the top and into heaven. The story of the Bible, however, signals the end of the road for the ladder approach to theology. It tells the story of the God who comes down to earth to save people from the compulsion to climb the ladder so that they may be free to live down-to-earth, trusting God's promise to take care of things above so that they may enjoy and take care of the creation, here and now and forevermore. In this chapter we put the story of the Bible in theological perspective and theology in biblical perspective.

---

[1]**Collegial** generally used to reference co-workers. However, literally, the term means forming into a community of college students, each sharing together responsibility in the group endeavor to understand and be understood. One of the premises of our course is that learning is a corporate, hands-on enterprise. I believe that each individual brings something important to our collegial enterprise. I also believe that the methods of study and discourse that you will learn this semester lead most effectively to deeper understanding. You will come to appreciate that these methods serve not only understanding the New Testament but understanding any text, whether contemporary or ancient, whether written, spoken, sung, or enacted. The key to success is active participation in the corporate enterprise.

Entering into Theological Discourse

Entering into the arena of theological discourse—reading, writing, speaking, listening, and thinking—is, says Kenneth Burke, like entering a room full of people who are in the middle of conversation.

> You come late. When you arrive, others have long preceded you . . . . In fact the discussion had already begun long before any of them got there, so that no one present is qualified to retrace for you all the steps that had gone before. You listen for a while, until you decide that you have caught the tenor of the argument; then you put in your oar.[2]

The contribution of those "others who have long preceded" us promises to greatly enrich contemporary theological understanding and conversation. The history of theological thought and conversation fills libraries. We have much to learn from those who have preceded us. It may be true, as Burke says; the subject matter of theology is so immense that no one person is qualified to trace all the steps that have gone before. However, we may note several historic contributors from the formative period of theology. Their contributions provide a sturdy foundation on which to build our theological conversation.

Greek Beginnings

Theological discourse dates back at least to the time of the Greeks. Among the Greeks theology originally referred to the **myths**[3] of the gods, as in the works of Homer (*Iliad*) and Hesiod (*Works and Days*).[4] Generally speaking, people derived what they knew about the gods and their involvement in human life from **mythology**.[5] The myths provided the source and basis of theological understanding and discourse. In part the corpus of myths functioned to explain why things are the way they are in human life; why, for example, it is never a good idea to defy one's fate. As well, the corpus of myths provided a basis to cultivate values—courage, temperance, truthfulness, humility, and loyalty, for instance. In this sense the myths taught people what values and beliefs to put

---

[2]Quoted in David S. Cunningham, *Faithful Persuasion* (Notre Dame: Notre Dame Press, 1990), 2.

[3]**Myth** in common English usage is often equated with "falsehood." Scholars, however, use the term differently. In scholarly usage a myth is a story that bears a truth that is always and everywhere true. Myths are valued, regardless of their historical authenticity, for their insights into life's realities, especially the human condition.

[4]There are many good studies of mythology in the classical era. I have found Edith Hamilton, *Mythology* (New York: Little, Brown and Company, 1942) to be a helpful resource; also H. D. F. Kitto's classic study, *The Greeks* (New York: Pelican Books, 1951).

[5]**Mythology:** a culture's corpus of collected stories about the gods. They explain why the world works the way it does. They provide a rationale for customs and observances, establish cultural rituals, and instill values and beliefs. Scholars distinguish myth from other narrative forms. For example, whereas myth is a story about the gods, a **legend** is a story about a human cultural hero. If the story concerns spirits or other supernatural beings, it is usually called a **folktale** rather than a myth.

their **faith**[6] in, what to believe about the gods, how to get their favor, how to live virtuously in relation to other people, and so forth.

© 2012 JupiterImages Corp.

For the Greeks, particularly under the influence of Plato and Aristotle, faith was not blind. It did not substitute for reasoning, understanding, and knowing. Rather, on the basis of what could be "reasonably" known from the myths, humans were justified to believe in the intangible realities of life—the danger of hubris, for example. The myths could also be used to commend a certain way of living, namely, the Greek way. For example, the Greeks knew well that Zeus took a dim view of people who lied and he might punish them by hurling a thunderbolt at them. Thus living honestly and truthfully—the Greek way—provided the way to remain in the favor of Zeus. But also, and not coincidentally, living honestly and truthfully contributed to the well-being of the social and political order. The Greek imagination is not alone. Contemporary culture continues to honor the centrality of truth in our life together. Regardless of what may have changed between the fifth century BCE in Greece and the twenty-first century of the contemporary world truthfulness remains essential to the promise of life together. The enduring quality of the myths is to be explained by their truthful depiction of human nature and the drama of life.

Christian theology—as the Princeton theologian and philosopher, Diogenes Allen shows in his masterful study, *Philosophy for Understanding Theology*[7]—has been since its beginning entangled with Greek thought. A brief survey of Plato and Aristotle on a couple of key issues illustrates for good and ill the entanglement. [8]

---

[6]In this sense **faith** means to put trust in. It is the beliefs that give shape and purpose to life. The question is: What are we justified to put faith in? And how can we know what faith will take us into the fullness of life? In this sense the question of faith is very much at the heart of our overarching questions: Who is God? What does it mean to be human?

[7]Diogenes Allen, *Philosophy for Understanding Theology* (Atlanta: John Knox Press, 1985).

[8]This examination of Plato and Aristotle is dependent on the insights of Oswald Bayer in *Theology the Lutheran Way* (Grand Rapids: Eerdmans Publishing Co., 2007), 3–13.

Plato (427–347 BCE)

Myths may be the source and basis of theological understanding, but, as Plato adamantly insisted, unexamined faith in the mythological "truths" leads to disaster. In the *Republic* **Plato**[9] strongly criticizes theology's sole dependence on poetic myths for its understanding of God and the human condition. He insists that theology should be a rational conception, based on disciplined study of reality. In other words, Plato views theology as a **metaphysical**[10] discipline. Plato admitted that the stories of the gods contained some truth. But they also in some respects misrepresented reality. Because it is difficult to unlearn ideas, those responsible for the well-being of social and political order must be taught sound ways of theological discernment. Plato had rulers specifically in mind. But, given our place in the democratic western world, we may expand his concern for sound education to include people like us—prospective parents, civic and business leaders, lawyers, doctors and nurses, teachers, engineers, and so forth. Plato's educational aims remain ours: to critically examine the myths of the culture, teaching those stories that encourage wisdom regarding the question of God and the human predicament.

For the social and political good of the human community theology must believe and assert, according to Plato, two truths about god: 1) god is good and 2) god is unchangeable. He strongly criticizes the Homeric notion that the gods are the source of evil as well as good. "The good is not the cause of all things, but only of the good; it is not responsible for what is evil and wicked" (379b; see 617e and *Theaetetus* 176b/c)."[11] If our city is to be well governed, he says in the *Republic*, "we must do all we can to prevent anyone, young or old, either saying or being told, whether in poetry or prose, that God, who is good, can cause harm or evil too anyone. To say that would be sinful, inexpedient, and inconsistent" (380b/c.)"[12] Social welfare and stability depend upon human confidence in the goodness of the gods. The rhyme and reason of life depend upon confidence that the gods do not act malevolently toward humanity.

Further, Plato asserts as the second premise of theology that the gods do not change. As Socrates asks Adeimantus, "Do you think that anyone . . . would willingly make himself worse . . . in any respect? . . . Impossible! . . . [Every god is the] best and [the] most beautiful possible, and abides forever simply in his own form."[13] God is timeless and not subject to change by any outside influences. The belief that the gods do not change provides the necessary stability for social and political order.

---

[9]See http://plato.stanford.edu/entries/metaphysics/ for more information about Plato. Samuel Enoch Stumpf's *Socrates to Sartre: A History of Philosophy* (New York: McGraw-Hill Book Company, 1966) is also an excellent introduction to Plato and philosophy in general.

[10]It is not easy to define **metaphysics**, especially as the discipline has been understood throughout the course of philosophical history. For our purposes we may define metaphysics as disciplined observations about the overarching realities of life based on general abstract reasoning. You may wish to consult http://plato.stanford.edu/entries/metaphysics/ for additional background on the question of metaphysics. You may also find helpful *Socrates to Sartre: A History of Philosophy*, by Samuel Enoch Stumpf (New York: McGraw-Hill Book Company, 1966), 48–159.

[11]Quoted in Bayer, *Theology the Lutheran Way*, 4.

[12]Ibid., 5. See also *Great Dialogues of Plato*. Edited by Eric Warmington and Philip Rouse. Translated by W. H. D Rouse (New York: The New American Library, 1956). The Republic, Book 2, p. 178.

[13]Ibid., 5. See also The Republic, Book 2, p. 179.

These two assertions function for Plato as the givens in theology. Whatever else theology may have to say, it must resonate with these two central and absolute truths. As one may readily appreciate from popular theological culture, these foundational Platonic truths have exerted enormous influence on contemporary theological thinking. Far and wide, they continue to be taken for granted in theological imagination today.

However, biblical imagination views God in a very different way. In the biblical view humans can only know about God what God chooses to let them know. Consider, for example, the story of Moses's encounter with God at the burning bush in Exodus 3. At one point in the encounter Moses asks for the name of God. In reply God declares "I am Who I am . . . the Lord, the God of your ancestors" (Ex. 3:14–15). In English the sound of God's name in Hebrew transliterates as Yahweh. In both Christian Testaments the name revealed to Moses remains the permanent and primary name for God. In the Old Testament Yahweh—I am Who I am—remains the primary name of God throughout the long story of faith. In the New Testament the primary name for God is Jesus. This name bears within it the claim that Yahweh saves.

Outside of and apart from Jesus and the story of Israel, however, God remains hidden. This is what Job learned in his encounter with God. In the wake of the disastrous collapse of his life Job and his friends speculate about the place of God in it all. In theology however speculation poses grave dangers in relation to God. Speculation never brings the human closer to God. In the case of Job, when the speculation turns to accusations against the fairness of God, God answers "out of the whirlwind: 'Who is this that darkens counsel by words without knowledge? . . . I will question you, and you shall declare to me. Where were you when I laid the foundation of the earth?'" (Job 38:2–4). Job is restored within the bounds of his humanity. Humans answer to God. God does not answer to humans.

© 2012 JupiterImages Corp.

In contrast to Plato's view, the God of the Bible is—all too clearly and all too frighteningly—the source of good and evil. God builds up and God destroys (Jer. 4). In the Bible human uncertainty and anxiety stem precisely from the reality that God creates evil and good (Lam. 3:38), life and death, light and darkness (Isa. 45:7), prosperity and disaster (Amos 3:6). In the biblical story of faith God conceals the truth and reveals the truth to whom he will in his own good time (Mk. 4:10–12). Humans, with respect to faith in God and with respect to their humanity, are completely at the mercy of God. Nonetheless, as clear as the biblical portrait of God is, Plato's view of God, perhaps for understandable reasons, has prevailed in popular imagination, even to the point that it continues to influence the way in which people read the Bible today. Under the influence of Plato, the biblical portrait of God to the contrary, people tend to bring these two absolutes into theological discourse—God is good and unchanging. But as Job learned in his whirlwind encounter with God, God refuses to be domesticated to the divine ambitions of humans: "Will you condemn me that you may be justified? Have you an arm like God, and can you thunder with a voice like his" (Job 40:8–9)?

Plato makes two additional contributions that have also had tremendous influence on the theological imagination of the west. The first is the dualistic distinction he drew between the visible, material, and temporal realm of sensory existence on the one hand and the invisible realm of pure, eternal ideas, on the other hand. The second closely relates to the first. Just as reality in general consists of the two worlds, invisible ideas and physical matter, so also the human consists of two components—body and soul. The physical body necessary to life in the material realm is subject to deterioration and death. The soul which originated in the eternal realm of pure idea will survive the death of the body and will return to the eternal realm where it will face posthumous judgment for the way that it has lived its bodily existence. The wise person, epitomized by Socrates, will continually examine material existence in light of the eternal truths, living a temporal existence that leads to eternal life. Contemporary moral imagination remains very much under the influence of Plato's religious outlook in this respect.[14] Think for example of the way in which people conceive earthly life as the means of proving oneself worthy of heaven. Or think of the distinction drawn between the lower carnal life and the higher spiritual life. Such thinking has its roots in the ancient soil of Greek culture.

Plato by no means exhausts the influence of the Greek ways of thinking on contemporary theology. His student, Aristotle, also has exercised enormous influence on the way in which contemporary people read the Bible and think about human life and God.

Aristotle (384–322 BCE)

© 2012 JupiterImages Corp.

Aristotle[15] may have disagreed with his teacher, Plato, in most every respect, but they were agreed about one thing. When it comes to theology, reason, along with Plato's two absolutes, provides the foundation for making sense of the world and living in harmony with the way things are, and must be, in truth. For Aristotle theology's project is to reason to the heart of reality, to understand what makes all reality go round and adhere. Theology, in other words, focuses on that which moves all things without itself being moved or affected by others. For Aristotle that "unmoved mover," is god. This is the reason why Aristotle approves the political order as conceived by Agamemnon in Homer's *Iliad*. "The rule of many is not good," Agamemnon declares; "let one be the ruler!"[16] Agamemnon quite clearly asserts who that one should be. But that point to the side, Aristotle concurs with Agamemnon's wisdom because it harmonizes with the truth of god and human existence. In other words for Aristotle theology is synonymous with metaphysics.

---

[14]See Stumpf's *Socrates to Sartre: A History of Philosophy*, pp. 65–73, for fuller treatment of the theme in Plato's philosophy. Also see Diogenes Allen, *Philosophy for Understanding Theology* (Atlanta: John Knox Press, 1985), 15–91.

[15]For a brief introduction to Aristotle see http://wsu.edu/~dee/GREECE/ARIST.HTM. See also Stumpf's *Socrates to Sartre: A History of Philosophy*. Also see Diogenes Allen, *Philosophy for Understanding Theology* (Atlanta: John Knox Press, 1985), 92–136.

[16]Quoted in Bayer, *Theology the Lutheran Way*, 7.

Plato and Aristotle then, in the "Greek way" of thinking, establish the question of god as the central question of theology. Theology seeks to know for the sake of human life the truth about god; the way god is in god's naked being. Christian theology agrees with the Greeks that the most fundamental question of theology is the question of God. The First Commandment sets forth the matter around which all else in theology and life revolves: "I am the Lord your God . . . you shall have no other gods before me" (Ex. 20:2–3). As Martin Luther explains,

> A god is that to which we look for all good and in which we find refuge in every time of need. To have a god is nothing else than to trust and believe him with our whole heart. As I have often said, the trust and faith of the heart alone make both God and an idol. If your faith and trust are right, then your God is the true God. On the other hand, if your trust is false and wrong, then you have not the true God. For these two belong together, faith and God. That to which your heart clings and entrusts itself is, I say, really your God.[17]

But while Christian theology may agree with the Greeks about the centrality of the question of God, the Christian approach to God, as we have already begun to anticipate, is markedly different in a number of respects. To that aspect of things we now turn our attention.

Christian Origins

© 2012 JupiterImages Corp.

The origins of Christian theology may be traced to the Apostle Paul. Paul was an influential missionary pastor of the early church. According to the Acts of the Apostles, Luke's story of the origin and expansion of the Christian movement, Paul's career is synonymous with the early history of the church. From chapter eight to the end of the story in chapter twenty-eight, humanly speaking, the story of the church features a host of individual efforts, but none more prominently than the ministry of Paul. By sheer volume, the rest of the New Testament confirms Luke's judgment about the influence of Paul in the early history of the church. Writings which bear the name of Paul comprise nearly half the New Testament, the Scriptures of the Christian church. In the course of the semester we will read a selection from Paul's letters. The reading will provide the opportunity to appreciate Paul's contribution to Christian theology, particularly at the point of our overarching questions: 1) Who is God? 2) What does it mean to be human? There are many places from his letters that could serve to summarize Paul's approach to theology, but perhaps none better than what he declares to the Romans: "Christ died for the ungodly . . . God proves his love for

---

[17]Martin Luther, The Large Catechism, *The Book of Concord* (Minneapolis: Fortress Press, 1959), 365.

us that while we were still sinners Christ died for us. Much more surely then, now that we have been justified by his blood, will we be saved through him from the wrath of God" (Rom. 5:6–8). For Paul the theological sun rises and sets on the crucified and risen Jesus. As he declares to the Corinthians, "Jews demand signs and Greeks desire wisdom, but we proclaim Christ crucified, a stumbling block to Jews and foolishness to Gentiles, but to those who are the called, both Jews and Greeks, Christ the power of God and the wisdom of God" (1 Cor. 1:22–25).

After Paul, the next great theologian of the Christian tradition in the formative era is Augustine of Hippo. Whereas Plato and Aristotle were philosophers Augustine was a pastor of the church. A philosopher in the Greek tradition bears similarity to a pastor in the Christian tradition. Both concern themselves with human life in harmony with the truth of God. However, there is an important difference. Whereas for the Greeks mythology and/or reason provided the basis and source of theology, for Augustine theology was all about reading the Bible in light of human experience.

Augustine (354–430 CE)

© 2012 JupiterImages Corp.

As we turn from the Greek to the Christian understanding of theology no thinker is more important than Augustine of Hippo. Augustine agrees with the Greeks that theology matters for human life, public and private. In his *City of God* he argues that the political and social well-being of the human community is at the mercy of good theology. As he puts it, "false opinions can arise and gods can be worshipped and believed who have no real existence at all" (6.5).[18] The most dangerous **idol** is in fact the idol of a particular political order. Augustine observes that the Roman historians praised the Roman order too highly. Not that anyone could blame them, for "they had no other and better city to praise" (3.17). Nonetheless it exposes the danger of **idolatry**. "If we offer our ultimate loyalty to the political community and its goods, we suppress the desire for god that marks the deepest reaches of our humanity."[19] Thus, as with the Greeks, the central aim of theology is to tell, in an intelligible way, the truth about God. As Paul also contended, faith must give intelligible witness "to its understanding. Otherwise, how will anyone know what you are saying? You will just be speaking into the air" (1 Cor. 14:8f.). For Paul, and the rest of the New Testament writers, to love God completely means to love God also with one's mind (John 6:69).

For Christian theology in the biblical tradition as it was taken up by Augustine, faith is not a substitute for reason and understanding. Neither the Bible nor Augustine would ever counsel, "you just have to believe," as though there is no evidential basis for faith.

---

[18] Augustine, *City of God*. Edited and translated by Gerald Walsh, et. al (New York: Doubleday and Company, Inc, 1958).

[19] Gilbert Meilaender, *The Way that Leads There: Augustinian Reflections on the Christian Life* (Grand Rapids: Eerdmans Publishing Company, 2006), 79.

On this point Christian theologians have no bone to pick with Plato and Aristotle. Reason and faith belong together. Exactly how they belong together remains an open question in Augustine's theology and beyond.

In sorting out the question of the relationship between faith and reason, Augustine begins with the question of happiness. With the Greeks he assumes that all people desire to be happy. But what makes for true and enduring happiness? From the Greeks Augustine had learned that true happiness lies in "what is *worth having*, and is *attainable . . . with security*, without fear of losing it against one's will."[20] With the Greek philosophers Augustine runs through the laundry list of what humans imagine will bring happiness—money, power, and pleasure. And with them he concludes that such things do not make for enduring happiness. God alone makes for true human happiness. As Augustine says, the human heart remains restless until it rests in the true God, the God who has freely given life.[21] The British apologist C. S. Lewis could well speak for Augustine when he observes that humans "are half-hearted creatures, fooling about with drink and sex and ambition when infinite joy is offered us."[22] In principle Plato and the Greeks would not disagree with Augustine's conclusion. However, over the question of the identity of God, Augustine and the ancient Greeks parted company. Their different views of God may in part be explained by the fact that they based their theological views on different "source books."

In the final analysis, what separates Augustine from Aristotle, Paul from Plato, is the evidential basis on which and from which theology speaks about God and the human predicament in relation to God. For Augustine theology begins and ends with the promise of God as witnessed in the Christian Scriptures. Theology, for him, in fact, is synonymous with reading and discussing the Bible. The Bible is the witness[23] to God's self-revelation in the story of Israel (Old Testament) and in the life, death and resurrection of Jesus (New Testament). The long story of God and God's creation as told in the Bible revolves around the twin questions: 1) Who is God? 2) What does it mean to be human? The Bible begins (Genesis) and ends (Revelation) with these two questions. They are never far from the heart of the story, nor from theological discourse.

According to the story of the Bible Augustine was compelled to turn upside down the relationship of faith and reason as it had been conceived by the Greeks. For Augustine faith precedes reason and provides the basis for reason to operate. Eugene TeSelle explains, Augustine "often quotes the Old Latin mistranslation of Isa. 7:9, 'Unless you believe you will not understand.' In this connection he makes three basic points: reason acting on its own will be frustrated; reason's path must begin with faith; and after it does

---

[20]Eugene TeSelle, *Augustine* (Nashville: Abingdon Press, 2006), 13.

[21]Augustine, *Confessions.* Translated with an introduction by R. S. Pine-Coffin (Baltimore: Penguin Books, 1961), 21.

[22]Quoted in Meilaender, *The Way that Leads There*, 3, from C. S. Lewis, "The Weight of Glory," in *The Weight of Glory and Other Addresses* (Grand Rapids: Eerdmans, 1965), 1–2.

[23]For the Christian tradition the Bible, Old and New Testaments, is the authoritative and normative basis of theology for two reasons, one historical and the other theological. From a historical point of view faith cannot get back to the events that comprise the telling of the Bible without going through the witness of the Bible itself. From a theological point of view, the Bible is authoritative because it witnesses to God's decisive and saving self-revelation in Jesus of Nazareth.

so, it can rise above mere faith and achieve a more lucid understanding."[24] Augustine may not have the final word on the place of faith and reason in knowing God but his insight that faith precedes reason deserves our consideration as we enter into the encounter with the God of the Bible.

In addition to Augustine two great theological traditions are of special interest. Both trace their origins to the sixteenth century. The Lutheran tradition traces its heritage to the Augustinian monk, Martin Luther. The Jesuit tradition traces its heritage to the sixteenth-century founder of the Society of Jesus, Ignatius Loyola. These traditions are of special interest because they set forth two fundamental and contrasting approaches to theological understanding.

Two Sixteenth-Century Theologians: Martin Luther and Ignatius Loyola

Martin Luther and Ignatius of Loyola were theologians of the sixteenth-century Catholic church. Both believed that the purpose of theology was to serve the generation and nurture of faith. Oswald Bayer describes Luther's approach to theology as a "pastoral theology marked entirely by the Word of Address that creates faith through the use of Scripture and thereby occasions the formation of passions."[25] John O'Malley describes Ignatius's approach to theology in similar terms: "We might call Ignatius's theology pastoral in the sense that it provides a religious vision, which gives distinctive shape to practices that help others in their faith."[26] While they may have similar views regarding the purpose of theology, Luther and Ignatius took different roads in their service to the church. Although they were contemporaries, they never met, but lived worlds apart. Luther was German; Loyola was Spanish. Not only did they live worlds apart geographically but they lived worlds apart theologically. An examination of their theological approaches to reading the Bible and Christian formation brings into focus the fundamental questions of theology: How can humans know anything about God with certainty? How are humans formed and shaped in their theological existence?

Luther was an Augustinian monk, priest, and university professor who was eventually **excommunicated** from the church. For Luther, however, excommunication did not mark the end of his theological career. In Wittenberg he continued to preach and teach at the university and in the city church. Through his considerable corpus of writings (54 volumes in English translation) as well as through his students, Luther's influence eventually spread to the far corners of the world and continues to shape theological imagination down to the present day. For Luther, as Oswald Bayer explains, theology is wisdom gained from experience, fostered by prayer, meditation on Scripture, and deep affliction. In other words for Luther theology is a passive life. Through these means— prayer, meditation, and affliction—God acts upon the believer to give and shape our true humanity. As meditation the disciplines of theology are the same academic disciplines

---

[24]TeSelle, *Augustine*, 15.

[25]Oswald Bayer, "Martin Luther (1483–1546)" in *The Reformation Theologians*, ed. Carter Lindberg (Oxford: Blackwell Printers, 2002), 52.

[26]John W. O'Malley, "Ignatius of Loyola (1491?–1556)," ibid., 301.

that inform any field of study—grammar, critical thought, and constructive discussion.[27] For Christian theology the field of study is the Bible as Word of God. God speaks to the believer only by means of the outward word of Scripture. The Bible tells the story of the way that God comes down to earth in Jesus to be "with us in the muck and work of our lives so much that his skin smokes."[28] By way of the cross of Jesus, God comes to save us by tearing us away from self-absorption to live freely by faith in God's promises and by love for the neighbor.

Ignatius of Loyola was an aristocrat who gave up the life of privilege to establish the Society of Jesus. Under the direction of Ignatius the Society of Jesus was, and is, dedicated to the propagation of the faith throughout the world and to the care of the faithful within the church. As Jerónimo Nadal, a close collaborator of Ignatius explains the Jesuit motto; "The world is our house" means that wherever Jesuits "can be sent in ministry to bring help to souls, that is the most glorious and longed-for house for these theologians." The "Jesuit way" of bringing help to souls, as O'Malley explains, is based on Ignatius's "own interior journey from conventional religious practice to a wholehearted commitment to follow the 'way' of Christ, a way culminated in a total surrender to God's love and will."[29] In his book, the *Spiritual Exercises*, along with the twelve volumes of his correspondence, Loyola, locates theology's field of study in the "interior life" of the believer. As he explains, "the Creator deals directly with the creature, and the creature directly with his Creator and Lord." The critical facility in the theological life is therefore the capacity to "discern" what the Creator and Lord of faith is saying to the believer. The *Spiritual Exercises* set forth then the "rules" by which the discernment is helped along. The most important "rule" is to apply the rules with discernment.

Not surprisingly these two approaches to theology make for very different expectations when it comes to reading the Bible. For Luther theological existence is a passive life. As the potter shapes the clay, God acts through God's Word to shape the life of his creation. The life of faith is an active life of loving service to the creation and prayer to God. As it is the nature of an apple tree to produce apples so it is the nature of faith to produce works of loving service. But life in relation to God is a passive life. God is the doer; Christians are the recipients of the doing.[30]

For Ignatius, on the other hand, theological existence is intensely active toward the goal of reshaping the self to be more open to God and neighbor. Ignatius views the Bible as the articulation of the ways pilgrims are to follow in making their way to God and the neighbor. On the basis of the concrete experience of life contemporary believers may imaginatively immerse themselves in the biblical narrative as they seek to find the way.

Let's take a closer look at these two approaches as they provide a basis for understanding the relationship between the Bible, theology, and Christian existence. Whatever

---

[27]Bayer, "Martin Luther," 51–66.

[28]Luther's famous characterization of Immanuel, God with us, is quoted by Bayer in his essay on Luther. Ibid., 51.

[29]O'Malley, 301.

[30]See for example Luther's explanations to the Apostles' Creed in the Small Catechism—http://bookofconcord.org/smallcatechism .php#creed—Each explanation of the three articles of faith revolve around the action of God. God, the Father, creates and sustains human life solely out of his gracious goodness, though we do not deserve it. God, the Son, saves from sin, death, and the power of evil through his innocent suffering and death. God, the Spirit, moves the human to faith through the preaching of the gospel.

their differences they are agreed that theology is a discipline in service of the proclamation of the Christian message that it may bring believers into communion with the true God and thereby make us free to be you and me.

Martin Luther (1483–1546)

© 2012 JupiterImages Corp.

For Luther the Bible tells the story of the relationship between God and humanity. So far, there is no controversy. Theologians from Thomas Aquinas (1225–1274) to Wolfhart Pannenberg (b. 1928), including Ignatius of Loyola, agree; the subject matter of theology is God in relation to humanity in the context of creation. The controversy arises over the way in which Luther characterizes the relationship between God and humanity. Theology, for him, is about humankind "guilty of sin and condemned, and God the Justifier and Savior."[31] The sin of which humanity is guilty expresses itself in the ingratitude for all that God freely gives out of God's goodness of heart. According to the biblical story, the gift of life and the gifts by which it is sustained come freely from God to all people, the pious and impious alike. The life of faith is a passive life. It is a life born of receiving and trusting God's promise to give and sustain life freely. Humans, however, refuse to trust the promise of the biblical God as the freely-giving God of creation. The sin of unbelief expresses itself by and through ingratitude for and blindness to the absolute and unconditional generosity of God.

Having lost faith in the unconditional graciousness of God, humans turn God into a bargain-barn deity with whom to trade good deeds for eternal bliss. Humans in turn curve inward in self-absorption, looking out for "number one" as though there is no one else to do it. When things are going along successfully as planned, humans take pride in deserving everything they have earned. When things do not turn out as planned, humans resentfully despair of life's unfairness. Either way, unhappily, self-absorption condemns humanity to an isolated life of slavish drudgery, greed, and anxiety, cut off from God and neighbors. It may be recognized by the aimless and joyless attitude that approaches life as a matter of "I have to . . . or else." It may be recognized as well in the regretful life of "could've, should've, would've." Or in the all-absorbing quest for identity, recognition, and acknowledgment. Or in the hapless life of the victim, like Adam and Eve in Genesis 3 after their fateful decision in the Garden, refusing to take responsibility but blaming everything under the sun for their troubles, including, and especially, the Lord God himself. This is the biblical portrait of the human, bound by circumstances, obligation, regret, and denial, and all the while intent on defending to the death the human freedom to decide its own fate. Humans are bound to not want God to be God,

---

[31] Quoted in Bayer's "Martin Luther," 53.

but wanting to be their own God. Instead of living happily as humans they live as unhappy gods.

This is the humanity for whom God in Christ comes. God comes down in Jesus to speak the truth about the human situation and to free humanity from its self-imposed bondage. As Jesus declares in John's story of God and humanity, "If you continue in my word, you are truly my disciples, and you will know the truth, and the truth will make you free" (John 6:31–32). The tragedy of the story is that the humans are blind to the truth of what Jesus says. In denial they seek to silence him in a permanent way. The good news of the Christian message tells of God's unwillingness to accept the human decision as the final word in the relationship. Jesus lives on the other side of death as the undying commitment of God to make a new beginning with creation.

The church through its preachers, teachers, and general membership exists to tell the story in such a way that listeners hear the story as their story. Where the story is told so that people hear the biblical story as the Word of God for them, there the church exists. The crucial thing is the telling and hearing in faith that the God who led Israel into the freedom of the Promised Land and raised Jesus from the dead is the only God for me. When believers have God in that way, or perhaps better to say, when God has believers in that way then they are free to live a truly down-to-earth human life. Now good deeds may be done in loving service of the creation and the neighbors with whom we share it. Christians are free from the sin of believing that good works are bargaining units to get God's favor and admittance to heaven. God has promised to take care of the believer's destiny in this life and the next out of the goodness of his divine and fatherly mercy.

Theology is the thinking that informs and directs the telling of the story that it may create faith in the hearers where and when it pleases God. The key to sound and salutary theology, as Luther never tired of emphasizing, is the recognition that the Word of God speaks to us as law and gospel, demand and promise. The art of the theology is the ability to distinguish law from gospel. "When I found this distinction between law and gospel," Luther observed, "I broke through."[32] It may seem a simple art but drawing the distinction is not as easy as one might imagine.

For Luther the distinction between law and gospel is not so much a distinction of content. The very same words can sound in the ears of the hearer as either law or gospel, or as a matter of fact, as both law and gospel in the same breath. The distinction is a distinction between powers or forces. It is a matter of what the spoken word does to a person. The law demands, accuses, provokes anxiety, enslaves. The gospel promises, absolves, comforts, liberates. All of this God gives out of his fatherly goodness and divine mercy. According to the linguistic pattern of gospel speech God speaks unconditionally to the creation: "*Because* I am the Lord your God, *therefore* I will take care of you as only God can do." Let's take a theological look at the first page of the biblical story from the perspective of law and gospel.

From almost the very first page, the Bible tells the story of conflict between God and humans over the question of who is in charge of human destiny. According to the story

---

[32] LW 54:442–3; Quoted in Bayer's "Martin Luther," 55.

of Genesis 2, God creates the human to enjoy and take care of the creation. God promises to look out for the humans as only God can do—"I am the Lord your God, you shall have no others." It is a word of pure promise. But for reasons difficult, if not impossible, to explain, humans are not content to live under God, at the mercy of God's promise. Instead of believing that God's promise makes of life a broad and pleasant paradise, humans fear that the promise of God imprisons them in the cave of ignorance. Refusing to entrust its destiny to God, humanity takes its destiny into its own hands. As the story unfolds in chapter 3 of Genesis, the humans desire to be as gods, to have the final say over their own destiny, to determine for themselves good and evil. That according to the story is the forbidden fruit (Gen. 3:4–5). It proves irresistible to the humans. They take and eat it. The hoped-for consequence fails to materialize however. Instead of being as gods, they see that they are naked and vulnerable humans. Now the humans experience the true God as a threat. They hide from their Creator. The very promise of God for them—"I am the Lord your God, you shall have no others,"—becomes an accusation against which they are compelled to make a defense. They point the finger of blame for their troubles at others. Adam blames the woman. In fact, he blames God who gave him the woman in the first place. The woman blames the serpent. The Lord holds them all accountable and they suffer the consequences of their "desire to be as gods."

This is our human bondage. Humans are bound by the refusal to have God as God. We desire to be as gods in charge of our own destiny. Instead of living as free and happy humans we live as anxious and unhappy gods. When humanity loses faith in God's promise to be for us, freely, we lose the human freedom to be for one another in the care of creation and the joy of life. In other words, we lose paradise. Lost paradise is not however the end of the story. In one of the most touching scenes of the whole Bible, the Lord God makes clothes to cover the shame of human unbelief and naked guilt (Gen. 3:21). God protects rebellious humanity from the cold consequences of paradise lost. In other words, humanity may have lost its innocence and faith, but it has not lost God because God refuses to give up on humanity. The story ends with the promise of God for humanity and not against it. As the New Testament tells the story, the gracious promise of Christ Jesus for humanity defines God as God seeks to be known.

Ignatius of Loyola (1491–1521)[33]

For Ignatius the Bible, or more specifically the life of Jesus as reported in the New Testament, provides the primary context for the spiritual examination of life. Under the direction of a spiritual guide who has been schooled in the *Spiritual Exercises*, **exercitants**[34] are led through a process of self-examination and meditation, with the culminating goal of deeper commitment to and more intense ordering of the life of faith—devotion to God and service to the neighbor. The *Spiritual Exercises*, written by Ignatius

---

[33] In this section of the chapter I am indebted to my colleague Michael Cook who at my request was kind enough to offer correction and insight to my understanding of Ignatius and the Jesuit mission. Of course any misconstrual of either the Jesuit mission or Ignatius that remains is due solely to my own continuing misperceptions.

[34] **Exercitants** is Ignatius's word for those who avail themselves to the Spiritual Exercises.

and based on his own experience, are designed as a systematic and disciplined method of meditation on the Christian life. H. O. Evennett, noting the intensity of focus involved in the meditations, characterizes them as a "shock-tactic" designed to concentrate the attention of the whole person—mind and heart—on the relationship to God and neighbor. The *Spiritual Exercises* are not however to be taken as a text in spiritual self-help. Rather, they presume the direction of a more experienced Christian. The *Spiritual Exercises* offer counsel to those who have, through the exercises, been moved to a deeper spiritual existence and who now seek to help others toward the same goal. The commitment to help others by "giving" Ignatius's *Spiritual Exercises* to others goes a long way in defining the purpose of the Society of Jesus.

© 2012 JupiterImages Corp.

From the beginning of the movement in 1540 to the present the *Spiritual Exercises* inspires the Jesuit mission. Wherever they have gone, the world over, and in all their activities—preaching, education, and works of mercy directed toward orphans, prisoners, and the sick, toward the neighbor in whatever need—at heart the aim has been to make known "the deeds of the Savior . . . for me" so that people would be turned outward toward others with the same commitment. The proven power of the exercises to move people to a richer spiritual existence lies in their capacity to lead people into intense meditation on the fundamental truths of the Christian message as it is set forth biblically. The key to the method of meditation is threefold: 1) flexibility in accommodating the person and circumstance of individual exercitants; 2) the discernment of spirits; and 3) thinking with the church. As John O'Malley explains, "In the *Spiritual Exercises* Ignatius created a road map based on his own interior journey from conventional religious practice to a wholehearted commitment to follow the 'way' of Christ, a way culminated in a total surrender to God's love and will."[35]

---

[35] O'Malley, "Ignatius," 301.

The exercises are designed to unfold in four stages, ideally spread over four periods, called "weeks." However, the exercises can be adapted, shortened or lengthened, depending upon the particular circumstance of the exercitant with and for whom they are undertaken. Whatever the precise period of time in which the exercises are undertaken their aim and foundation is set forth clearly by Ignatius in the "Principle and foundation." Here Ignatius states that "Man is created to praise, reverence, and serve God our Lord, and by this means to save his soul . . . . From this it follows that man is to use [all things on the face of the earth] as much as they help him on to his end, and ought to rid himself of them so far as they hinder him as to it."[36]

The first "week" of the Exercises begins with meditation on sin and hell, encouraging examination, confession, and eradication of one's faults. The second movement begins with the call of Christ the King and focuses on the life of Christ from his Nativity through the course of his public life up to the point of the final, fateful trip to Jerusalem. With special attention to the narratives of Jesus's life exercitants are encouraged to "elect" to promote the kingdom of Christ in and through their chosen walk of life. Meditating on the passion of Christ in the third movement of the Exercises, exercitants continue to cultivate and strengthen their resolve to promote the way of Christ and the values of the kingdom. The fourth movement of the Exercises centers on the revelation of the love and glory of Christ made known in his resurrection. Throughout the course of the Exercises the goal is to cultivate what Joseph de Guibert, an early Jesuit brother, has termed the "spirituality of service." In pursuit of the goal the role of imagination could scarcely be underestimated. The Exercises provide the occasion for exercitants to imagine themselves in the story world of the gospel narratives that the "world" of the story may affect them intensely with the "spirituality of service."

In contrast to Luther who emphasized the passive nature of hearing and being affected by the Word of God as spoken in and through the biblical word, Ignatius emphasized the active reflection necessary to hearing the Word of God in the context of one's own life. As Ignatius emphasized, the Spiritual Exercises provide the opportunity "to conquer oneself and regulate one's life without determining oneself through any tendency that is disordered."[37] For Luther humans are at the mercy of another who will speak the good news of God. As Paul asked, "How are people to believe in Christ as God unless someone proclaims him?" (Rom. 10:14). Whatever else is to be made of this difference, the two approaches agree that the encounter with the Bible as the Word of God is for the sake of creating humans content to live down-to-earth, trusting God to be God and seeking to be of some earthly value to creation and the neighbors with whom it is shared. Whether both approaches lead to the intended outcome is a question that can only be answered in the actual course of the encounter with the New Testament.

---

[36]Ignatius of Loyola, *The Spiritual Exercises*. Translated by Elder Mullan. Edited by David L. Fleming. (St. Louis: The Institute of Jesuit Sources, 1978), 22.

[37]Ibid., 20.

The Place of the New Testament in Theological Discourse

Our examination of the Lutheran and Jesuit approaches to reading the New Testament illustrates the place of theology in the enterprise. For both traditions theology is the thinking that goes on between the ear and the mouth, between what has been heard as the good news of God for me and speaking the good news of God for others.

I want now to turn our question upside down. To this point we have been thinking about the place of theology in reading the Bible. Now we want to focus attention on the place of the New Testament in theological discourse. The New Testament may be used, and frequently is used, to end theological discussion. One quotes the Bible as though it were the final word in the matter under discussion—"The Bible says . . . that settles it, end of discussion." Of course the Christian community has no access to the truth of God except in and through its Scriptures. In that sense the Bible must be granted the last word in theological discourse. However, before the tradition grants the last word to the Bible it also views the Bible as the basis and beginning of theology. The Bible generates theological discussion. Theology is, as Augustine emphasized, conversation between lived experience and the Word of God as spoken in the words of Scripture. Our course honors Augustine's emphasis. We study the New Testament to open up discussion and lead more deeply into richer understanding of human life in relation to God, creation, neighbor, and self.

Entering into Theological Discourse

One does not have to be a member of the church in order to enter theological conversation, nor does one have even to be particularly religious. In fact, one does not have even to believe in God. The New Testament does not require faith as a prerequisite. In fact, many convictions of faith are represented in the theological conversation, including the conviction that God does not exist. When thoughts and opinions about God, along with other matters related to faith's commitment and conviction, come to expression we have entered upon theology. From whatever stance one enters theological conversation, when the New Testament is in play, the promise is that you will not be left the same by the end of it.

Theology, a Volatile Discipline

One does not have to participate very long in the theological conversation before discovering that things can become volatile. Reading the Bible together has as frequently led to division and strife as to solidarity and harmony. People agree and disagree in their opinions and convictions, in fact, sometimes people agree and disagree strongly. Because people tend to have strong theological opinions, conversation frequently becomes strident. Theological discourse has sometimes led to strife, schism, and war. For this reason we have grown understandably reticent about participating in theological conversation.

It is one of those areas, perhaps the last remaining area of public or ecclesial life, which is to be avoided in the company of others—whether strangers or friends—with whom there is risk of encountering difference of opinion. Nothing has the potential to blow up in our faces like reading and discussing the Bible.

© 2012 JupiterImages Corp.

Many proposals have been made to contain theology's explosively destructive potential. Some propose that theology be banished from public discourse. Others propose to resolve theological conflict by agreeing to disagree. Some propose to bracket out the explosive question; Who is God? Still others seek to limit theological conversation to private or sectarian groups of the like-minded, in which all the members of the group are known ahead of time to agree with one another.

But theological discourse has proven difficult to avoid or contain. Despite the public resolve to keep religion out of politics the more it pops up in elections from dog-catcher to president. Or think of the hot-button moral issues of the day—abortion and gay rights, for example. In part the debate about such issues seems to be driven by differences of underlying theological understandings. Or think of the challenge of communities of different religious persuasions—Christians, Muslims, Jews—living together in ever closer proximity to one another. If we can't avoid theology perhaps some attention to manners and method might prove useful and even fruitful in the ongoing theological conversation.

An Approach to Theological Discourse

On the other hand, it is difficult to imagine that it is possible for people to enter into theological discourse apart from commitment to particular "givens." In this aspect of things perhaps a modest proposal might provide a way forward. Presuming that people enter theological discourse with certain "givens" does not require us also to presume that these "givens" must necessarily be brought into the discussion as "take-it-or-leave it" assertions. What if we were to imagine theological discourse as an enterprise in which the participants seek to make persuasive arguments for their "givens"? Such an orientation would provide a framework for discussion constructed of questions designed to uncover warrants, presuppositions, implications and consequences. In this sense theology is the same as any other intellectual discipline taught in the university. Like those disciplines theology wants to know:

A. What is the warrant for the position being advanced?

B. What presuppositions does the position presume? Are the presumptions valid? What defines valid?

C. Who benefits and at whose expense?

A Christian Perspective on Participation

Preparing to enter theological discussion might give a person pause. It may present us with all sorts of challenging issues, but theological reflection cannot be escaped for long. We are all theologians whether we want to be or not. Whenever we think about broken friendships, what we are meant for, why "bad" things happen to "good" people, and so forth we are thinking theologically. The question then is not whether we will enter into theological reflection but rather the question is how good our theological reflection will be. Our purpose in this course is to collegially cultivate a manner of reading, thinking, and discussing that leads to deep and fruitful theological discourse.

I find encouragement in observation of the New Testament writer, Luke. Luke contends that in theological matters we remain a people of the way. As the travelers in the last chapter of his Gospel, we remain on the road to understanding. One of my teachers expanded on Luke's meaning. His words have stuck in my imagination: In the course of making our way in theological discourse, he said, "[w]e have only our wits, some suggestions offered by the host of witnesses that surround us, and the promise that the spirit of truth will lead us into the truth." Our enterprise, he concluded, "is more like sailing than like building cathedrals. We don't have control over the elements—just enough to navigate in the face of surprising shifts of wind and changed water conditions. Some would perhaps hope for more stability but for sailors bedrock is where sunken ships lie."[38] For me, as a Christian theologian, that has seemed promising enough to sustain participation in theological engagement with the neighbors that life has given.

---

[38]"Your Word is Truth," in *Shaping the Scriptural Imagination: Truth and Meaning, and the Theological Interpretation of the Bible.* Edited by Shane Berg and Matthew L. Skinner (Waco: Baylor University Press, 2011), 19.

Study Questions:

1. In what ways are the Greek and Christian approaches to theology similar and dissimilar?

2. Compare and contrast Luther and Ignatius in their approach to theology.

3. What is the place of theology in the study of the New Testament? What is the place of the New Testament in theological discourse?

4. What do you understand to be the "absolute claims" of Christian theology? What "absolute claims" do you hold as you enter into theological conversation with your colleagues in the class? What are your "givens"?

5. What do you understand to be the difference between assertions and arguments?

6. In your own words summarize what you take away from this chapter.

7. Formulate the questions that emerge for you from your study of the material in this chapter. Be prepared to offer one or more of the questions for reflection and discussion in class. Explain why these questions emerge out of the chapter and what you believe to be at stake in them.

Terms:

In addition to the definition as derived from the use of these terms in the paper you may want as well to consult the *Oxford English Dictionary* as you develop an understanding of the key terms of this chapter.

Metaphysics	Absolute claims
Mythology	Human Predicament
Warrant	Theology

For Further Study:

In addition to the works cited in the endnotes, the themes of this chapter may be explored in more depth by consulting:

Augustine. *On Christian Doctrine*. Translated by D. W. Robertson, Jr. New York: Macmillan Publishing Company, 1958. In this work Augustine sets forth his principles for reading the Bible and theological discourse in a Christian context.

Mark Ellingsen. *The Richness of Augustine: His Contextual and Pastoral Theology*. (Louisville: Westminster John Knox Press, 2005).

David S. Cunningham. *Faithful Persuasion.* Notre Dame: University of Notre Dame Press, 1991. Cunningham describes a rhetorical approach to theological discourse.

Ignatius of Loyola. *The Spiritual Exercises: A Literal Translation and A Contemporary Reading.* Edited by David L Fleming. St. Louis: The Institute of Jesuit Sources, 1978. In this classic work the founder of the Society of Jesus describes his program for reading the Bible and spiritual formation.

Martin Luther. The Small Catechism and The Large Catechism in *The Book of Concord.* Edited by Robert Kolb and Timothy J. Wengert (Minneapolis: Fortress Press, 2000). In these classical works Luther sets forth the basics of Christian theology.

Martin Luther. "Preface to the New Testament." *Luther's Works.* Volume 35. Philadelphia: Fortress Press and St. Louis: Concordia Publishing House, 1960. Views the good news of Jesus Christ as the center of the New Testament proclamation.

Chapter 3

The New Testament as Literature

The most obvious thing about the New Testament could perhaps go without saying. It is words on the page. While it may go without saying it provides the basis for launching the contemporary encounter with the New Testament. Presumably someone put these words on the page to be read. The vitality of the encounter with the New Testament will to some extent depend upon the reader's appreciation of these writings as literature. The New Testament has not always been appreciated as literature in the same way that Homer's *Iliad* or Mary Shelley's *Frankenstein* is regarded as literature. But literature, according to the dictionary, is "a writing in prose or verse regarded as having permanent worth through its intrinsic excellence."[1] As words on the page I can't imagine a better description of the New Testament. The challenge posed to readers is the challenge of developing the facility to appreciate the "intrinsic excellence" of the New Testament literature.

It may seem strange to suggest that the New Testament is literature in the same sense that the *Iliad* is literature or in the same way that *Frankenstein* is literature. In fact the suggestion may even seem sacrilegious. Most of us have learned to think of the Bible somehow on a higher plane than ordinary literature. Among Christians, in fact, the Bible does have a higher status than all other books. For Christians the New Testament, as one division of the Holy Bible, belongs to *the* book above all books. As the **Scriptures**[2] of Christian faith these writings are set apart from ordinary writings as the sacred Word of God. Over the centuries readers have found these writings to be truthful, and therefore authoritative, with respect to the question of God and human self-understanding. It may be conceivable to speak about the Christian understanding of God and human life apart from the Bible, but it would be exceedingly foolhardy. What could we reliably know about the God of Christian faith apart from the Bible? Nothing. For this reason, in the view of the Christian church the Bible provides the authoritative, normative basis for theological discourse about God and human life.

---

[1] *Random House Webster's College Dictionary*. Edited by Carol G. Braham et al. (New York: Random House, 2001), 776.

[2] For our purposes **Scripture** designates religious writings that are authoritatively valued and used to illuminate the faith and life of the community. While many communities of faith have Scripture they do not use and value the same writings as Scripture. For the Muslim community the Koran constitutes Scripture. For the Jewish community it is the Tanakh. The Christian community regards the Bible as Scripture.

© 2012 JupiterImages Corp.

Not only is the Bible regarded as the normative basis for theological discourse about God and human life in relation to God, but in these writings the church expects to hear the Word of God. By means of the biblical word, according to the expectation of the church, God addresses God's Word to and for faith. As Karl Barth, an influential theologian of the twentieth century, has observed,

> The fact of the canon tells us simply that the church has regarded these scriptures as the place where we can expect to hear the voice of God. The proper attitude of preachers does not depend on whether they hold on to a doctrine of inspiration but on whether or not they expect God to speak to them here.[3]

The judgment of the church regarding the place of the Bible in contemporary theological life is borne out in many people's experience. The encounter with the Bible has in fact shaped their theological imagination in decisive ways. Learning to read the Bible as literature promises to deepen one's appreciation of its power and authority as the Word of God. Thus again here is the question I wish to pose to and with students of the New Testament: What if learning to read the Bible in the way that you read ordinary literature were to enrich your experience of the Bible precisely as the Word of God? Of course such a question cannot be answered in the abstract. It is the sort of question that can only be answered by actually giving it a try. Do these writings work as literature? And if so, does reading them as literature deepen the encounter with these writings as Word of God?

---

[3]Karl Barth. *Homiletics*. Translated by Geoffrey Bromiley and Donald Daniels. (Louisville: Westminster John Knox Press, 1991) quoted in Elizabeth Achtemeier, "The Canon as the Voice of the Living God." *Reclaiming the Bible for the Church*. Edited by Carl Braaten and Robert Jenson. (Grand Rapids: Eerdmans Publishing Co., 1995), 119.

The Challenge

Developing the facility to read the New Testament as literature will prove challenging for at least two reasons. First, for many of us our prior exposure to the Bible has tended to convince us that the Bible is best understood as a collection of "lessons" that teach what's right to do and believe. In the Sunday worship of the church, for example, the readings from the Bible are frequently introduced as "lessons." Whether by preachers at the pulpit or teachers in the classroom, the individual lessons for Christian faith and life are extracted and considered apart from their original literary setting. The individual readings are seldom considered as parts of the larger literary whole from which they have been taken. It will require patience and imagination as we seek to put back together literary works that have been broken up into bits and pieces.

The second consideration which makes reading the New Testament as literature difficult is simply that these writings are quite old. They are very much products of their time in antiquity. If students have experience reading the writings of Homer or Sophocles or some other ancient writings they will appreciate the challenge of reading the New Testament as literature. To read the New Testament as literature requires patience as we learn to take these writers on their own terms. As an early and influential teacher of mine insisted, "If you want to read the letters of Paul, the least you could do is learn his language."[4] It was the beginning of a lifelong study in ancient Greek. It may not be necessary for all readers to learn the original language of the New Testament. There are many fine, trustworthy translations available. However, taking these writings on their own terms will involve learning to appreciate the literary forms, strategies, and conventions as their authors practiced the art of writing in their own time. Taking these writings on their own terms will also involve developing historical imagination to understand how they may have sounded in the ears of first-century readers.

The New Testament as a Collection of "Lessons"

Most university students—whether coming from public or parochial secondary school, whether frequently in the Sunday worship of the church, or never been in attendance at church—are familiar with the parables of Jesus's teaching. Among the more famous parables is the Parable of the Sower (Mark 4:1–20). Before reading further in this chapter, take a few minutes right now to read the Parable of the Sower and write a brief paragraph in response to the question: Why does Jesus tell this parable?

---

[4]The observation was made to my classmates and me in our first course in Paul's theology at the very beginning of our seminary education by our teacher, Roy Harrisville.

Processing the Mini-Assignment

Most students will have responded to the question by explaining that the parable encourages us to "cultivate our soil" so that the word of Jesus may produce a bountiful harvest of good works in us. Such an interpretation of the parable makes no use of the narrative setting in which the parable has been told. Readers have heard as though the parable were directly spoken to them. Seldom does it even occur to students to read the parable as part of the larger story in which it is spoken by Jesus to his narrative audience at a particular time and place. Reading the parable as part of the larger story narrated by Mark will make a world of difference to the way in which readers hear it.

The Parable of the Sower in its Markan Context

When reading Gospel **lections**[5] in narrative context, the challenge is to read the individual parts in connection with one another, to read the whole in light of the parts and the parts in light of the whole. The interpreter seeks to detect patterns and themes that emerge as the individual narrative units are connected to one another. In this case the interpreter seeks to determine the place and function of the parable in Mark's larger story of Jesus. In other words: 1) Why does Jesus tell the parable at this particular point in the story? 2) What is the point of reference between the parable and the events of the narrative? What does the parable make clearer? 3) What is the reaction of the narrative characters to the parable? 4) Why does Jesus teach in parables?

Before answering these questions we must first consider what happens within the story of the parable. According to Jesus's interpretation of the parable (vv. 13–20), the sower sows the word (v. 14). The various soils represent the way in which the word is received among its hearers (vv. 15–20). As it turns out, the seed does not fare well in most of the soils where it has been sown. Along the hard path "Satan immediately comes and takes away the word" (v. 15). Among the thorns, the cares and riches of life choke out the seed before it reaches fruition (v. 19). On the rocky ground, the seed fails to produce a harvest because it lacks sufficient depth for the seed to put down roots deep enough to sustain it during times of persecution and trouble (v. 17). In most soils nothing comes of the sower's efforts. However, in the deep, rich soil the word bears a remarkable harvest—thirty, sixty, and a hundred fold (v. 2), quite a miraculous yield given the standards of the day. Normally first-century farmers could expect a fivefold yield; a seven and a half to tenfold yield would be considered a bumper crop. But the seed of the parable gets thirty, sixty, and a hundredfold yield. Remarkable!

Now that we have reviewed what is reported in the story of the parable we are ready to consider our questions. What is the point? Why does Jesus tell the parable at this juncture of the story? Most readers will be inclined, correctly, to understand the parable allegorically. Accordingly, readers identify the sower with Jesus. In fact the suggestion

---

[5]Lection is a select portion of text. Readings from the Bible selected for the public worship of the church are frequently referred to as lections. They are as well sometimes referred to as a pericopes.

has been planted in the mind of the reader by the narrator. Earlier in the story the Markan narrator announced that in the ministry of Jesus the kingdom of God has come near (1:14–15). The Parable of the Sower, along with the other parables of chapter four, addresses the relation between the ministry of Jesus and the fullness of the kingdom that has drawn near. Together the two other parables of the chapter—the Parable of the Scattered Seed (vv. 26–29) and the Parable of the Mustard Seed (vv. 30–32) —make the point that the kingdom consists of two phases: the planting time and the harvest time. The Parable of the Sower in this context focuses attention on the planting time, the time of Jesus's ministry.

Jesus tells this parable at a time in his public ministry when it begins to appear that his efforts on behalf of the kingdom seem to be headed for failure. While he continues to attract enthusiastic crowds from among ordinary people, ominous clouds begin to form over his career. The Pharisees criticize Jesus for keeping company with tax collectors and other riffraff, undeserving of God's favor (2:15–17). His family concludes that "he has gone out of his mind" (3:21). Scribes who have come down from Jerusalem accuse him of being possessed of a demon (3:22). The Pharisees have conspired with the Herodians to "destroy him" (3:6). The list of his own disciples includes one who will betray him into the hands of his enemies (3:19). Opposition against Jesus is anchored in the same judgment about him. He has been conducting himself as though he were God on earth, above the law (2:23–28), not subject to normal standards governing humanity (1:21–28), doing what only God is authorized to do (2:3–7). For that he will be rejected, condemned, and destroyed, as he himself anticipates (see 8:31; 9:31; 10:29).

The parable acknowledges, to the narrative audience as well as to the readers of the story, that while the Word of Jesus will not find a fruitful reception everywhere, in the end his efforts will be vindicated by a miraculous harvest. His ministry will produce fruit for the kingdom of God. Just in the way that the tiny mustard seed produces in the harvest time the greatest of all shrubs, so the ministry of Jesus will produce a harvest of fruit, thirty, sixty, and a hundred fold. In this sense the parable provides for readers of Mark's Gospel a synopsis of the plot. Among the narrative audience of Jesus the reader can identify characters whose reception is like the hard soil. From the very beginning the Pharisees, scribes, and Herodians do not give Jesus a chance. Without ever suffering second thoughts or change of heart they reject and condemn Jesus from the very first encounter (see 2:6; 3:6, 22). There may even be a sense in which the disciples of Jesus themselves are like the hard soil. The better they get to know Jesus and the longer they are with him the more obdurate they become toward Jesus. At one point the narrator is at such a complete loss to explain the disciples' lack of understanding that he can only conclude that their hearts have been hardened (6:52). Jesus himself questions them in the same vein: "Do you still not understand?" he asks them. Seeming to be at a loss to explain how they could be so dense, he is driven to ask, "Are your hearts hardened? Do you have eyes, and fail to see? Do you have ears, and fail to hear?" (8:17). By examining other characters of the narrative according to the images of the parable, we could continue to demonstrate the way in which the parable serves as a plot synopsis regarding the success of Jesus's efforts on behalf of the kingdom of God, but for now enough has been said to illustrate the way in which interpretation proceeds to read the parable as part of the larger narrative.

Even as students begin to see that the text of Mark might work as a story, still taking this approach to reading Mark and the rest of the New Testament will prove challenging. Old habits die hard. It will be difficult to resist the deeply ingrained habit of reading the individual lections in isolation from the larger literary whole. As we said earlier, most students to this point in their lives have had a lifetime of reading the individual narrative units—the sayings and doings of Jesus—as lessons which admonish believers to live in one way or another. Readers, for example, tend to take the parable of the sower as an admonition to cultivate their "soil" so that they will produce a rich harvest of good works. Even when I point out that in telling the parable Jesus issues no admonition, students insist upon reading an admonition into it. It is common for students to ask why would Jesus tell the parable if he wasn't exhorting the reader to do something. Even when I point out that the image of inert soil is hardly conducive to the suggestion that believers ought, or even can, do something, to improve their receptivity, still students tend to take the parable as a lesson in cultivating their "spiritual soil." As the educational theorist, Frank Smith, has pointed out, learning has as much to do with forgetting as with acquiring new knowledge and skills.[6] Studying the New Testament in a fruitful way will require that students unlearn old approaches in the interest of taking up the more promising literary approach.

Getting the Message

If reading the New Testament is like reading any other literature, it will be profitable to think about the experience of reading. The first thing to be said: reading is work! Reading demands work because texts do not speak for themselves. Texts are lifeless words on the page; they require readers to give them voice. In the course of giving voice to a written text readers must make all sorts of interpretive decisions about how to understand and connect the words to one another. In other words, getting the message of the New Testament is as much a function of what readers get from the text as what the authors have put into the text.

The traffic between reader and text runs in both directions. As George Steiner points out, "To read well is to enter into answerable reciprocity with the book being read . . . to read well is to be read by that which we read."[7] In other words, reading involves not only what readers make of the text, but also what the text makes of readers.

The aim of cultivating knowledgeable and sensitive readers for the New Testament is therefore twofold. In the first place we aim to help readers of the New Testament become more aware of the interpretative decisions that we make in the course of giving voice to

---

[6]*The Book of Learning and Forgetting* (New York: Teachers College Press, 1998).

[7]George Steiner, *No Passion Spent* (New Haven: Yale University Press, 1996), 6.

the text. In the second place this study guide suggests an approach to reading the New Testament that leads to a respectful, rich, and sensitive encounter with the Word of the New Testament.

© 2012 JupiterImages Corp.

Generally speaking, getting the message of a text is relative to the difficulty of the text and to the experience and preparation of the reader. When I read *Sam I Am* to my grandchildren it is fairly effortless on my part. Having read Dr. Seuss to two generations of children, to my daughters and now to their children, plus plenty of other children in between, I am fairly adept at "reading out" the message. That is, not only am I adept at getting the message of Dr. Seuss but I am pretty good at performing the message of Dr. Seuss, reading it aloud in a way that engages their interest and enjoyment of the sound of the words on the page.

However, when the tables are turned and my grandchildren begin to read Dr. Seuss to me the "getting of the message" becomes a demanding work. For beginning readers merely decoding the sound of the words on the page is an arduous work. And that is to say nothing of putting those words on the page together in the playful and delightful flow of phrases and sentences, à la Dr. Seuss.

I can sympathize with their struggle. Even as an experienced reader of some sixty odd years I still find "getting the message" of some texts, say for example Shakespeare's *King Lear*, a demanding work. But I stick with it, for to me reading Shakespeare is a labor of love, much like reading the Bible. I have been hooked on Shakespeare since the first reading of *Romeo and Juliet* in high school. Over the years I have grown ever fonder of these plays. The more informed I have become about the "world" of Shakespeare, both inside and outside of his plays, the richer and more rewarding the encounter with his works. Of course the real payoff of becoming an informed reader of Shakespeare occurs in the enjoyment of taking in and being taken in by the performance of the plays.

As an avid reader of Shakespeare I have been drawn into the worlds of these various dramas and the drama of the worlds has gotten inside me. "All the world's a stage, / And all the men and women merely players: / They have their exits and their entrances; / And one man in his time plays many parts . . ."[8] And the playing of our "many parts" is greatly enriched by seeing them played out in the dramas of Shakespeare. So, what have we learned about reading in general that will serve to cultivate informed and skilled readers for the New Testament, so that we may have a richer experience as we travel around in the world of the New Testament?

The Work of Reading

The work of the reader may be summed up in one word, interpretation. To interpret, according to the *Random House Dictionary of the English Language*, means to "bring out the meaning by performance."[9] Reading a book is similar to musicians reading a musical score. In order to perform the notes on the page musicians must make all sorts of interpretive decisions. It is the same with reading words on the page. Whether it is actors on the stage of the Globe, or the old grandfather in the rocking chair with his grandchild on his lap, or a student alone in the library reading silently for an audience of one, interpretation culminates in performance, giving voice to the text for hearers.

© 2012 Jupiterimages Corp.

Whether reading Dr. Seuss or Shakespeare or the Bible, interpretation involves three moves. First, readers must collect and decode the data that the author has given them to work with. In addition to the words on the page, readers must also take into account the way that the words have been set down in relation to one another. That is, readers must take into account such things as grammar, syntax, genre, rhetorical strategies, and

---

[8]Quotation from *As You Like It*, 2.7.

[9]*The Random House Dictionary of the English Language*. Second Edition. Edited by Stuart Berg Flexner et al. (New York: Random House, 1987), 998.

literary conventions. Second, in order to make sense of the data readers have to make connections and fill in gaps. Third, on the basis of making connections and filling in gaps readers then draw inferences in the interest of reconstructing the sense of the text. An example will help to clarify what's involved in each of these steps.

In the first chapter of Mark's Gospel the narrator introduces a character into the drama with these words: "John the baptizer appeared in the wilderness, proclaiming a baptism of repentance for the forgiveness of sins . . . Now John was clothed with camel's hair, with a leather belt around his waist . . . He proclaimed, 'The one who is more powerful than I is coming after me'" (1:4, 6, 7). Without much effort most readers infer from verse 7 that John's role in the story has to do with heralding the coming of Jesus. While such a conclusion may be correct, it leaves many details of the narrative unaccounted for. In what sense, for example, is Jesus to be understood as "one more powerful"? What is the meaning of a "baptism of repentance"? What is the meaning of "sin" in the phrase, "forgiveness of sins"? What's to be made of the description of John's attire—"camel's hair shirt and leather belt around his waist"?

For the purpose of our illustration let's focus on the data about John's clothes. Of all that the narrator could have told the reader about John it must seem peculiar that he provides this description of John's attire. What do these descriptive details add to the way that readers see John? Most contemporary readers will be at a loss to explain the significance attached to John's clothing. In other words, there is a gap in the contemporary reader's understanding of the text. Did ancient readers have background knowledge that would have served to make sense of these details of the narrative? Ancient readers familiar with the Scriptures of Israel would have found John's description reminiscent of a biblical hero from the days of King David and his descendants.

According to the story from Israel's Scriptures, Ahaziah, king of Israel, had been injured in a fall. Instead of praying to the God of Israel for recovery, Ahaziah sent for the help of Baalzebub, the god of a neighboring kingdom. When the Lord God got wind of what Ahaziah had done he sent his prophet Elijah to intercept the messengers of Ahaziah with the news of God's displeasure: "Is it because there is no God in Israel that the king seeks comfort from Ekron? Tell the king to get comfortable in the bed he's made for himself because he won't be getting up from it." When the king got the message he asked by what sort of man it had been delivered. The messengers said that it was a guy dressed in a camel's hair shirt and leather belt. On the basis of the description King Ahaziah recognized at once that Elijah the Tishbite was the source of the message (2 Kings 1:1–8). Elijah was a prophet of the Lord God; a word from his lips was as good as a word straight from the lips of the Lord God himself. The point is that the king recognized the identity of Elijah on the basis of the description of the prophet's attire. By the way that Mark has told his story, readers are led to recognize John for who he is, Elijah. Depicting John as Elijah has special significance for Mark's story. Elijah, according to the Jewish Scriptures, was expected to return from heaven to herald the coming of the Messiah (see Malachi 3 and 4).

This example is not an isolated instance. On every page of the New Testament readers find themselves in the position of having to make connections and fill in gaps in order to make sense of what they are reading. Frequently the gaps are filled in and connections are made intra-textually (within a text) as well as inter-textually (between texts).

The challenge of filling in gaps and making connections intra-textually (within a text) involves reading the parts in light of the whole and the whole in light of the parts. Consider this example from the Gospel According to St. Mark. In chapter 12 the narrator tells of a time in the Temple when Jesus observed a poor widow contributing all that she had to the Temple treasury. Apparently Jesus takes the offering of the widow as a teaching moment for his disciples. He assembles them and explains, "Truly I tell you, this poor widow has put in more than all those who are contributing to the treasury. For all of them have contributed out of their abundance; but she out of her poverty has put in everything she had to live on" (vv. 43–44). That Jesus has made the poor widow an example seems clear. But of what is she an example? Most readers will be inclined to see her as an example of generosity, devotion, and sacrificial giving. It is not surprising. That is exactly the way in which the sermon of the church has taught people to read the story. Whether preachers are from a liberal or conservative tradition, Protestant or Catholic, they present the poor widow of Mark 12 as an example of generosity and devotion. It is understandable. In the context of raising money for the church the poor widow emerges from the biblical story as an example of generosity and devotion to be emulated.

However, when read in the context of the Markan narrative, the story sounds much different. In the context of Mark's story the poor widow contributes her last two pennies, not to the church, but to the treasury of the Temple. In Mark's story the Temple stands condemned by God. In the very next episode of the story Jesus predicts that in the near future God will make rubble of the Temple (13:2). Further, Jesus drives out the Temple administration of his day because they have turned God's house of prayer into a "den of robbers" (11:17). The Temple authorities are condemned because in addition to using their position for personal advantage, they "devour widows' houses" (12:38–40). Thus in Mark's narrative the reader cannot fail to appreciate that while this poor widow may be an example of pious devotion and sacrificial giving, just so she is an example of a poor widow whose piety is exploited by Temple leaders who stand condemned for their infidelity to God. She gives her last two pennies to a condemned institution, of no value as a house of prayer, the purpose to which God had originally dedicated it. Read in narrative context the story sounds very different than it might sound in the context of a preacher's sermon during the season of the church's annual financial campaign.

This is not to say that readers will necessarily prefer the version of the story that emerges from reading it in narrative context. In fact readers frequently resist that version of the story which views the woman's offering as an example of the way that the Temple leaders exploit poor widows and abuse their office. It is commonplace for students to offer interpretations of the story that in some way see redemptive value in the offering of the poor widow. It is worth asking what such efforts say about us and about interpretation. Interpretation is not limited merely to "objectively" making out the meaning of a text. Interpretation proposals, in addition to giving voice to the text, are also designed to comfort readers, protect vested interests, and advance the rhetorical agendas of interpreters. In that sense reading the New Testament reveals as much about readers as it does about the meaning of the words on the page.

Readers of course do not come to the text with a blank slate. Our ideas of what a text is about come, actually, from two sources: 1) the text, of course, but also 2) from the prior knowledge—namely, past experiences, hunches, convictions, presuppositions, sense of reality, and so forth—that is rattling around in our minds as we read. Our reading of the New Testament is not only influenced by the words on the page, but also by previous readings to which we have been exposed. It is understandable, perhaps even virtuous, that we are not inclined to give up prior understanding easily. So when should the reader allow new readings to overrule or replace old readings? How can we know when we should change our minds about the meaning of what we read? Part of the answer will lie in what is at stake in various ways of reading. What and whose interest do various interpretive proposals serve? In addition to asking how interpretive proposals use the data of the text, a good question by which to sort out why certain interpretive proposals appeal to us is to ask how they affect us. Thus as we read the New Testament we continually seek to maintain clarity about what informs our interpretive proposals.

To recap: our method, or way of reading, involves three steps—1) Collect the data—words, grammar, conventions—that the author has given the reader to work with; 2) make connections between parts of the text, seeking to detect patterns, themes, character and plot development, and fill in gaps; 3) draw inferences—in the interest of reconstructing with the author the sound of the words on the page.

Genres of the New Testament

The reader encounters essentially three **genres** in the New Testament—narratives, letters, and apocalypse. Let's take a closer look at the works that comprise each of these divisions and how our reading method applies to them.

Letters

There are essentially two groups of letters in the New Testament: 1) the letters under the influence of the Apostle Paul and 2) the general **epistles**.[10] In chapter one we briefly described the content of the individual letters. This chapter provides insights about the most promising way to read these writings of the New Testament.

---

[10]Epistle is another term for letter.

Letters Under the Influence of Paul

Undisputed Letters of Paul	Deutero-Letters of Paul	Pastoral Epistles
1 Thessalonians	2 Thessalonians	1 Timothy
1 Corinthians	Ephesians	2 Timothy
2 Corinthians	Colossians	Titus
Galatians		
Philippians		
Philemon		
Romans		

Scholars refer to the letters under the influence of Paul as **occasional** letters. The designation draws attention to the fact that they were written to address circumstances within the recipient communities. Reading the letters is like hearing one side of a telephone conversation. Until you know what is being said at the other end of the line it is difficult to understand what you are hearing. Thus to understand the letters readers must reconstruct the circumstances within the communities which have occasioned the writing of the letters. The main source we have for reconstructing the situation in the recipient community is the letter itself. We can picture the challenge in this way.

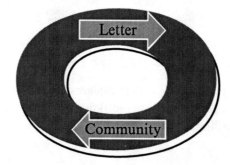

In other words, we read the letter with an eye to collect data that will help us to reconstruct the situation within the recipient community so that we can better understand the way in which the letter addresses the situation. In this sense reading the letter involves the reader in a circular process. Scholars refer to this phenomenon as a **hermeneutical circle**.[11]

---

[11] **Hermeneutical Circle** refers to the process by which interpreters seek to make sense of a text by viewing the individual parts in light of the whole and the whole in light of the individual parts. In the case of the Pauline Epistles the circle is formed between the text of the letter and the reconstructed situation of the recipient community which has "occasioned" the letter.

As all letters, the letters under the influence of Paul were written as a substitute for personal presence. In that sense letters employ many of the same **rhetorical**[12] conventions and techniques used in oral/aural communication. Paul in particular proves himself especially adept in the use of the Greek form of argumentation. In fact he was such a master in the use of the letter form to accomplish his aims that other leaders of the early church followed his example, as the so-called **Pseudo** or Deutero-Pauline letters and the Pastoral Epistles show. When reading these writings of the New Testament, it is helpful to approach them as to their form as letters and as to the structure of their argument.

The Epistolary Form of Paul's Letters

For the most part Paul adopted the standard form of a Greco-Roman letter. In Paul's day the standard letter consisted of four parts: Opening Salutation, Wish for Well Being, Body, and Closing Salutation. The one innovation that Paul made on the form was to expand the Wish for Well Being into a Prayer of Thanksgiving for the faith and life of the recipient community. Beyond that the letters of the New Testament bear the marks of Christian identity in a number of ways. For example, the recipients are greeted with the grace and peace of God by which they are united in the community of faith.

Focusing on the individual elements which comprise the **epistolary structure** of the letter, readers are able to collect data that is helpful in the course of reconstructing the circumstances that have occasioned the writing of the letter.

Opening Salutation
Prayer of Thanksgiving
Body
Closing Salutation

For example, the Opening Salutation consists of three elements: sender, recipients, and greeting. By noting the way in which the sender identifies himself, the way in which the recipients are characterized, and the nature of the greeting, readers can gain insight into the relationship between sender and recipients. Consider, for example, the Opening Salutation in Galatians (Gal. 1:1–5) and Philippians (Phil. 1:1–2). By comparison to the Philippians the Opening Salutation in the Galatians letter is polemically expanded. Paul draws a line under the fact that he has his apostleship, his authority to speak for the Lord, not from a human source, but directly from God (Gal. 1:1–2). Further, Paul notes that he is not alone in his understanding of the Christian message. "All the members of God's family who are with" him endorse what he has to say in the letter. The usual

---

[12]**Rhetoric** will be more fully defined in chapter 5. For our present purposes we may define rhetoric as the means by which authors seek to persuade and shape their audience.

apostolic greeting—grace and peace—is expanded to emphasize the saving sacrifice of Christ who gave himself to liberate believers from the present evil age. Combined with the fact that Galatians is the only letter of Paul which lacks a Prayer of Thanksgiving, readers of the letter might have the impression from the Opening Salutation that there are deep tensions in the relationship between Paul and the Galatian Christians. Our point is that by paying close attention to what is written and the way in which it is written readers can so-to-speak read between the lines to see the circumstances that surround the letter. Insight into the occasion of the letter helps the reader to better make sense of the content of the letter.

The same is true with respect to the body of the letter. In the body, or main section of the letter, the sender develops the message in light of the prevailing circumstances of the recipient community. In reconstructing the argument of the letters two insights are crucial. The first comes from Greco-Roman influence. Not surprisingly Paul—along with those who came after him—structured his argument according to the standard form and rules that governed making arguments in his world. From the Stoics, a popular school of philosophy at the time, **rhetors** had learned the art of making arguments. The idea was to clearly state the thesis of the argument and then to lead the **interlocutor**, or the discourse partner, logically along the way from the thesis to the conclusion, anticipating and answering any possible misunderstandings, objections, and questions that might arise along the way.

The Rhetorical Structure of Paul's Letters

The term, **diatribe**, by which the Greek method of argument was known, was taken from the method itself. Diatribe is based on two Greek words, *dia* (along) and *tribus* (path). The diagram below pictures the diatribe.

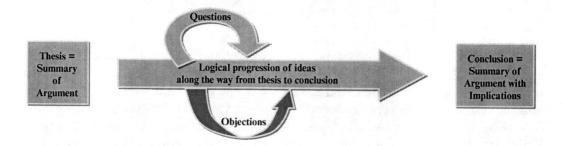

The elements of the argument provided for the logical development from thesis to conclusion. The chart on the next page shows the logical steps in moving from thesis to conclusion. These steps of course were not always taken in the same order. Nor was every step necessary to every argument. The chart however gives the student an idea of what to look for in tracking the argument or the rhetorical structure of Paul's Letters.

Exordium	Introduction	Cultivates openness and sympathy
Narratio	Narrative	Explains the nature of the disputed issue in social, moral, and historical context
Propositio	Statement of Case	Logically lays out basic propositions of the argument
Probatio	Support and proof	For Paul support and proof are generally derived from the Jewish Scriptures
Refutatio	Rebuttal	Refutes opposing points of view
Peroratio	Conclusion	Summarizes the case with emotional appeal for assent

Paul's Letter to the Romans provides an excellent example of his style of argumentation. This letter appears to have been written by the Apostle toward the end of his career as a self-introduction to his person and message in the interest of soliciting the support of the Roman congregation for the planned expansion of his missionary endeavors into the west (15:22–24). Thus the letter qualifies as the fullest extant expression of Paul's understanding of the Christian message. In 1:16–17 Paul states the thesis of the letter. These verses of the letter are frequently referred to as the gospel in miniature. From this opening statement of his message he then leads his interlocutor along the way to the conclusion, which he sets forth in 3:21–24 and defends with proof from Scripture (4:1–25). The rest of the letter draws out the implication of the Christian message for the life of faith.

The second insight that is important for understanding the argument of the letters is their use of the Jewish Scriptures as the evidential basis of the argument. At the time when the letters of the New Testament were written the Jewish community read its Scriptures as a compendium of God's Word. These writings provided the basis from which faith sought to make its way in understanding and life. How the connection between the present circumstance and the Word of God as preserved in Scripture was to be made was governed by certain rules of appropriation. These rules were known as **middoth**. For our purposes two rules are important to note. First, there is the analogy based on greater to the lesser: If this greater reality is true then how much the more is the lesser reality also true. So for example according to the argument of the Romans Letter, if it is true that Abraham, the father of faith, was justified by faith, then how much the more is it true that the children of Abraham are also justified by faith (Rom. 4). Second, there is the analogy based on like wording. Because the story of Abraham in Genesis 12–17 is about the faith and Abraham it may be appropriated as support for Paul's argument about the efficacy of faith in Christ's justification of sinners (Rom. 4).

So reading the New Testament letters under the influence of Paul for today is learning to read them through the lens of the situation of their first recipients and in light of the forms and logic which were employed in their composition.

General Epistles

We have been referring to the second group of letters that comprise the New Testament as the general epistles because, unlike the letters under the influence of Paul, these letters address the Christian community in general. While to a greater or lesser extent they share the letter format it might be better to characterize them as sermons or essays on issues of general interest to the church at large. James, for example, under the theme that faith without works is dead exhorts believers to be not just hearers but also doers of the Word. Hebrews presents Christ as a compassionate savior and moral example to be emulated in relation to the neighbor. First Peter is a meditation on the meaning of baptism in the light of suffering for the faith. The letters are attributed to, but very likely not written by, leaders of the church associated with Jerusalem, the original center of Christian community. They come from a time toward the end of the first century and are among the last writings to be included in the New Testament collection. Even though in these ways the General Epistles are very unlike the letters under the influence of Paul, nonetheless, readers will find it profitable to take the same general approach to them.

James
Hebrews
Jude
First and Second Peter
First, Second, and Third John

Narratives

The second major division of writings in the New Testament consists of narratives. Four narratives—Matthew, Mark, Luke, and John—are devoted to telling the significance of Jesus for faith. One of the narratives, The Acts of the Apostles, actually the sequel to Luke's story of Jesus, tells the story of the formation and expansion of the Christian movement. In chapter 2 we introduced each of the narratives; here our focus centers on reading them.

Narrative is defined as a series of connected events, either written or spoken. E. M. Forster, a noted novelist of the twentieth century, famously illustrates the difference between the mere rehearsal of a series of events, on the one hand, and a story, on the other hand: "The king died and then the queen died," he offered, is not a story because there is no connection between the two deaths. However, when the narrator provides a connection, "The king died and then the queen died of grief over the death of the king," now we have a story.[13] The important thing in a story then is the way in which the

---

[13]See *Aspects of the Novel* (New York: Harcourt, Inc., 1955), 86.

events are connected. How the narrator connects the events is as important as what the narrator tells.

Stories are told for many reasons: to entertain, to inform, to explain, to give identity, to instruct, to move to action, and so on. The narratives of the New Testament are not exhausted by any one purpose in the telling. They are complex and function at a number of levels all at once. The reader's encounter will be enriched by an exploration of how the narratives function at various levels and in various ways. For our purposes we concentrate attention on the ways in which the New Testament stories of Jesus and the early church function to inform and move readers or hearers by creating a narrative world into which readers are drawn.

These narratives inform in two ways: historically and theologically. Historically they paint a portrait of Jesus and his significance for the faith of the believing community which arises from the encounter with him. The relation of these stories to the actual events in real time is complex. We address this aspect of things more fully in the chapter on the New Testament as history. Theologically, the New Testament narratives focus on two fundamental questions: 1) Who is God? 2) What does it mean to be human? This aspect of things we address more fully in the chapter on the New Testament in theological discourse. In this chapter our focus centers on how the narratives function to create a narrative world into which readers are drawn.

We may begin by observing that the narratives of the New Testament unfold at two levels: the **story level** and the **discourse level**.[14] At the story level the narratives report what transpires within the narrative world of the characters. At the discourse level the narratives draw readers into the encounter with the big ideas of the story.

Discourse Level = What happens to readers of the narrative
Story Level = What happens to characters within the narrative

When reading a narrative readers are engaged at both levels. At the story level readers work with the author on the basis of the data of the text to reconstruct <u>what</u> happens to <u>whom</u>, <u>when</u>, <u>why</u>, <u>where</u>, and <u>how</u> within the world of the narrative. In addition to collecting the data that the author has given the reader to work with we must also make connections, fill in gaps, and draw inferences as we put the data together to reconstruct the narrative. At the discourse level readers take up the question of how the claims or ideas of the narrative play in the world of the reader.

---

[14]Students who wish to explore the distinction between the two levels of the narrative will find Seymour Chatman, *Story and Discourse: Narrative Structure in Fiction and Film* (London: Cornell University Press, 1978) to be helpful.

What is Narrative Analysis?

Narrative Analysis is a critical technique designed to foster reader familiarity with a narrative by focusing attention on the elements and style of a story. For our purposes we have defined story as a purposeful recital of events designed to shape the sense of self, community, and world. Our aim is to understand how the story works at the two levels. At the story level we seek to understand the parts of the narrative in relation to the whole and the whole on the basis of the parts. That is, by viewing the parts in relation to the whole and the whole on the basis of the parts we seek to establish the narrative point of view as it can be made out from the way in which the story has been constructed by the author and told by the narrator. As well, we seek to uncover the tone and atmosphere of the story as it is revealed in the words used to tell the story. We seek also to understand the character, plot, and setting function in the telling of the story. All of these considerations are addressed as literary questions with literary answers.

Title/Author/Narrator/Point of View/Tone:

Analysis begins with consideration of the **title**. Titles are important because they suggest what a narrative is about and thus lead readers to certain expectations. The titles of the individual works within the New Testament pose a challenge. Frequently titles of the various New Testament writings have been applied by someone other than the original author. For example, the Gospels of the New Testament—Matthew, Mark, Luke, and John—were so named by Irenaeus, a second-century scholar and bishop of the church. While readers may find it interesting and valuable to think about what such titles reveal about the writings, interpretation is better served by looking to titular clues in the respective piece itself. For example, many interpreters have taken Mark 1:1 as the title of the Second Gospel: "The Beginning of the Good News Story of Jesus, the Christ, the Son of God." The verse provides the elements to guide interpretative investigation into the piece. What does it mean to call Jesus, Messiah and Son of God? In what sense is the story good news? In what sense is Mark's narrative only the beginning of the Jesus story?

Whether the piece under investigation gives up a title or not interpreters need to develop a working title. Sometimes the interpreter may be unable to decide on a title for the piece until some preliminary understanding of the piece has been achieved. Further, one's sense of an appropriate title may change as the interpretative work proceeds (see questions 1–4 below).

Similarly, **authorial ascription** is tricky. Frequently we do not know the identity of the historical personage who has composed the writings of the New Testament. More often we have to content ourselves with the **"implied author"** of the piece, that is, the author as he/she can be made out from the piece itself (see question 5). The question of **narrator** is crucial. More than anything else the narrator establishes the point of view from which the story is told. It is the narrator's voice that one actually hears in reading a piece. The narrator, like the other characters of the story, is the creation of the author. Thomas Mann speaks of the narrator as the "whispering wizard." By that he means to draw attention to the way in which the narrative voice shapes the reader's experience of the narrative, which occurs in a variety of ways. Study which seeks to understand the effect of a piece (how it works to make its point with the audience) will of necessity be interested in the question of the narrator's role in the story (see question 6).

Finally, there is to consider the question of **tone**. The tone of the story is established by the language that is used to express attitudes toward the subject and toward the audience. Tone may be formal, informal, intimate, solemn, somber, playful, serious, ironic, condescending, and so forth. In some measure the tone of the story determines how the reader / hearer feels about the story (see question 7).

Questions related to Title, Author, Narrator, and Tone

1. Does the text provide a title? If so, what is it? Does it seem fitting? Why / why not?

2. How would you title this piece? Why?

3. What expectations does the title raise with respect to what the piece is about?

4. What elements of the title require interpretation, or explanation?

5. How would you characterize the author (historical, implied?) especially with respect to his/her theological outlook?

6. What voice does the narrator presume—dramatized or undramatized; first or third; omniscient or limited omniscience; reliable or unreliable? How does the narrator shape the reader's experience of the piece?

7. Identify language that functions to determine the tone of the piece. Describe the tone.

Setting, Plot, Character

Aristotle contends that in order to have a story you have to have three elements: setting, plot, and character. These three elements serve then as the basis to collect the data which the author has given us to work with, as well as the means to get inside the art of a narrative, to understand how the story has been constructed and works.

Setting

The setting of a story indicates the time and location in which the reported events take place. Setting often changes in the course of the narrative. Settings function in a variety of ways in a narrative. Setting may function to create atmosphere around the reported events. In chapter five of his story, for instance, Mark reports in vivid detail a particularly fierce storm at sea which terrifies the disciples. Setting can also contribute to conflict in a narrative (the Temple in chapters 11–16 of Mark's story provides a fitting setting for the escalating dispute between Jesus and the religious authorities of the Jewish community). Sometimes setting may even function symbolically. For example, in John's Gospel, the narrator relates that one night a certain Pharisee, Nicodemus, engages Jesus in conversation (3:2). It is clear from the introduction of John's piece that night/darkness is associated with evil/opposition (1:5). Sometimes understanding symbolic associations related to geo-political references requires background knowledge which modern readers may not have, thus expansion of our background knowledge is necessary. For example, the first eleven chapters of Mark's story take place in Galilee, a locale associated, for various reasons, with dubious religious movements, practices, and beliefs (see John 1:46).

Questions Related to Setting

1. What is the setting of the piece? Cite textual references which inform your answer.

2. Does the setting change in the course of the story?

3. Does the setting function symbolically? Are associations or value judgments made with respect to the setting?

4. Is there a relationship between setting and structure of the narrative?

Characters

Narrative characters may be flat (unchanging) or round (changing). The reader comes to know them by 1) the way in which the narrator/author describes them, 2) the way other characters in the narrative perceive them, 3) as well as by the report of what they think, say, and do. On this basis, characters are defined by certain traits. In Mark's story, for instance, Jesus emerges as a man of action. His word has power to bring about that of which he speaks. Jesus, according to Mark's portrait, evidences a wide range of character traits. He is a man of his word. He has a sense of humor. He is loyal, also abrasive, determined, authoritative, charismatic, exasperated, impatient, and so on.

It is through the interaction of the characters that the plot (see below) of the story moves forward. In the biblical narratives not all the characters are human, but nonetheless they play a role in the story. In Mark's story God, Satan, and demons play crucial roles in the narrative.

Also, in the biblical narratives, similar to the chorus in Greek theater, some of the characters are corporate. For example, in Matthew's story there seem to be three groups of characters: Jesus and his disciples, the Pharisees and the Religious Authorities, and the crowds.

Questions Related To Character:

1. Who are the significant characters? Why are they significant?

2. Describe the characters. Are they portrayed sympathetically or unsympathetically?

3. Who are the protagonists and who are the antagonists? On what do you base your judgment?

4. What do particular characters contribute to the story?

5. Which characters matter to the reader's experience of the story? How and why?

Plot

As Aristotle explained in the fourth century BCE, plot refers to the arrangement of a story's events so as to connect them into a narrative or a purposeful telling. The events of the story include, of course, the actions of the protagonist and how these actions affect other characters. Not only are other characters in the story affected by narrative developments, but so as well are readers. As M. H. Abrams points out in *A Glossary of Literary Terms*, "The plot in a dramatic or narrative work is the structure of its actions, as these are ordered and rendered toward achieving particular emotional and artistic effects" (127). E. M. Forster draws the distinction between story and plot on the basis of causality. "The king died, and then the queen died" is a story. "The king died, and then the queen died of grief" is a plot.

Questions Related to Plot

1. What event(s) forms the beginning, the middle, and the end of the story? Be sure to provide specific textual references.

2. Note the setting in which the event—forming the beginning, middle, and ending—is reported.

3. What is the climax of the story?

4. Is the story "heavily plotted" (each incident occurs closely related to the next one; one incident leads to the next) or episodic (episodes do not seem to be interrelated).

The Two Levels of the Narrative—Story and Discourse

The two levels of the narrative refer to 1) what the characters know and experience (Story Level), and 2) what the readers know and experience (Discourse Level). At the

Story Level, interpretation, by observing literary conventions and strategies, seeks to track and illuminate the experience of the characters and the development of the plot. The Discourse Level, or idea level, of the narrative refers to the conceptual themes of the piece. At the discourse level of the New Testament readers are drawn into theological consideration of God's identity, the human predicament, the nature of salvation, faith, sin, and so on.

As David Rhoades has pointed out, the New Testament narratives operate with certain **standards of judgment**,[15] by which subordinate points of view (those of other characters) are evaluated. That is, for example, Mark regards Jesus as the Christ or Messiah of Israel (1:1; 8:29). All other points of view are evaluated in light of that dominate point of view, as articulated by the narrator throughout the Gospel. Interpretation at this level, by observing rhetorical strategies, seeks to track and illuminate the experience of the reader in the course of engagement with the thesis or big ideas of the particular writing under investigation.

Questions Related to the Story Level

1. See the questions above in connection with setting, character, and plot.

Questions Related to the Discourse Level

1. What are you feeling and thinking by the end of the piece?

2. How do you react to the portrayed events and characters?

3. How does the piece portray the human situation in relation to God?

4. How does the piece depict God?

5. How does the piece conceive faith?

6. Describe the "implied audience" of the piece.

7. What sort of experience does the piece provide for its audience/readers?

8. Does the piece seem to be creating a readership?

9. Does the piece seem to be cultivating a point of view toward life, God, religion, etc.?

10. What is the theological/sociological/political point of view (prejudice[s]) of the piece?

---

[15]See *Reading Mark: Engaging the Gospel* (Minneapolis: Fortress Press, 2004), 44–62.

Apocalypse

The final genre represented in the New Testament, apocalypse, has only one entry, the Revelation to St. John, the last book of the Bible. Revelation has generated a great deal of confusion and controversy among its readers. Because of the controversy surrounding it the work did not find a permanent place in the canon of Christian Scripture until the fourth century, relatively late in the period of the canon's formation. Even so, controversy and confusion about the content and the style of the book continue unabated down to the present day. To many readers Revelation's damning judgment of unbelievers, enemies of the faith, and unfaithful Christians (see Revelation 15–16) contradicts the saving promise of Jesus as it is represented throughout the rest of the New Testament. Other readers have taken Revelation as a timetable of the end of days. Proposed timetables have seldom agreed. And many predicted endings have come and gone without incident.

We may not be able to propose an approach to Revelation that completely resolves the controversy and confusion. We can however propose an approach to Revelation that promises to see and hear Revelation for what it is. In his preface (1:1–4) the author of Revelation characterizes the genre of the work in threefold fashion: 1) apocalypse, 2) prophecy, and 3) open letter. Our approach arises from and honors each of these designations.

Apocalypse means literally to uncover and expose. By the time that John wrote his book the term, among Jews and Christians, had become associated with a particular type of literature. Such writings were designed to show beneath the outward realities of history the purposes of God. Typical features of such literature were heavenly visions, symbolism, numerology, and myth. Generally speaking from the visionary vantage point of the literature, history could be seen as a battle between the forces of evil and the forces of God. In fact, according to the visionary vantage point history could be divided into two ages. In the old age evil dominates; in the new age the forces of evil will have been destroyed and God will have established his perfect rule of good undisputed. This apocalyptic view of history provides the outline for the story of Revelation. The first 11 chapters envision the intensifying power of God's enemies. Evil manifests itself in the powers that be. The unrighteous prosper. The righteous suffer. The suffering of God's righteous saints summons God to act. Just as it seems that the righteous will be annihilated by the draconic forces of evil, God raises up a Savior who defeats and destroys the forces of evil in one final decisive battle. The final chapters of Revelation (12–22) envision the new age in which the wicked are punished and destroyed, while the saints of God share the everlasting blessing of God's goodness—"God himself will be with them; he will wipe every tear from their eyes. Death will be no more; mourning and crying and pain will be no more, for the first things have passed away . . . But as for the cowardly, the faithless, the polluted, the murderers . . . their place will be in the lake that burns with fire and sulfur" (Rev. 21:3–4, 8).

This vision of God's rule then is the prophecy that is to be proclaimed in the church. **Prophecy** in classical Jewish thought was understood to be the living speech of God delivered by a human agent. The prophets were as the great Jewish scholar, Abraham Heschel, characterized them, the mouthpiece of God. Prophecy applies to Revelation in the sense that the message does not originate with John. Rather it is the message of God which John merely writes down for the benefit of the seven churches to which the piece is addressed (1:17–20).

This brings us to the final consideration with respect to the genre of Revelation. The vision of God's purposes has been revealed to John for the sake of these flesh and blood Christians who lived in the seven communities named as recipients for whom the message is intended. In the open letter to the seven churches (Rev. 1–4), each community is encouraged to "listen to what the Spirit [of God] is saying to the churches" (see Rev. 2:7, 11, 17, 29; 3:6, 13, 22).

These insights into the genre of Revelation have a number of implications for contemporary readers. In the first place it should be evident that historical considerations will be in play as we seek to read Revelation through the lens of Christian experience in the final decade of the first century. The symbol, myth, and numerology of the book will need to be made out as it might have been understood in the Greco-Roman world of that time. As well, narrative analysis will be in play. As with the Gospels, we have in Revelation the drama or story of God's purposes as they can be made out beneath the outward circumstances of history. At the same time, in as much as Revelation aims to move believers to public lives of faithfulness, rhetorical considerations will be in play. What strategies and conventions has John employed in the course of seeking to accomplish the central aim of his writing? Finally, theological considerations will be in play in as much as the drama at its heart concerns what it means to have as God, "the Almighty Alpha and the Omega . . . the first and the last, the beginning and the end" (see Rev. 1:8; 22:13).

Summing Up

In this chapter on the New Testament as literature we have shown that our approach will enrich the encounter with each of the literary types which comprise the collection of writings. Reading the New Testament on its own terms requires contemporary students to collect the data which the various authors give us to work with, make connections and fill in gaps, in the interest of drawing inferences toward reconstructing the message. In this sense interpretation of the New Testament is like the game of chess. The terms of play are fairly straightforward and relatively easy to grasp. But gaining facility and useful background information is as long and as deep as a lifetime, in fact many life times, in as much as interpretation builds off the insights of generations of readers who have gone before.

Terms:

Sacrilege

Scripture

Lection

Gospel / gospel

Interpretation

Tanakh

Middoth

Plot

Setting

Character

Discourse Level of Text

Narrative Level of Text

Study Questions:

1. Define literature as it is used to describe the New Testament. Recall the dictionary definition as set forth in the first paragraph of the chapter.

2. What is the promise of reading the Bible as literature?

3. What is the challenge of reading the Bible as literature?

4. What is the relationship between reading and interpretation?

5. Name and describe the three steps of interpretation.

6. Explain how the steps of interpretation apply to reading the letters of the New Testament, the narratives of the New Testament, and the Apocalypse.

For Further Study:

William A. Beardslee. *Literary Criticism of the New Testament.* Philadelphia: Fortress Press, 1970. Explores the literary art and form of the New Testament genres.

Robert M. Fowler. *Let the Reader Understand.* Minneapolis: Fortress Press, 1991. Based on his study of Mark's Gospel, Fowler focuses attention on what happens to readers when they read the Bible.

Frank Kermode. *The Genesis of Secrecy.* Cambridge: Harvard Press, 1979. As the single-most important challenge to interpreters of the Bible, Kermode explores the tendency of interpreters to impose their reading of the biblical text by cunning and violence.

Amos N. Wilder. *The Bible and the Literary Critic.* Minneapolis: Fortress Press, 1991. In this collection of essays, Wilder explores the intersection of theology, aesthetics, and hermeneutics.

Chapter **4**

The New Testament as History

Beginning students want to know whether the New Testament can be trusted to give a reliable account of reported events as they have transpired in real time. For many students the question makes or breaks interest and investment in the study. It is understandable. The central event, which the New Testament reports, occurred at a particular time and place in ordinary history. According to the New Testament God comes in the historic person Jesus of Nazareth as the way, the truth, and the life of humanity. So the question—"Is it true?"—is completely understandable. It is also a more complex question than typical students appreciate at the outset of their university study of the Bible.

At the outset of the study students answer the question differently from one another. Some students take the historical veracity of the New Testament on faith. Other students incline to dismiss the reliability of the New Testament because they have difficulty trusting the objectivity of its version of reported events. Many students I suspect find themselves somewhere between the extremes. In the first part of this chapter we will illuminate what asking and answering the question of the New Testament's historical integrity involves. In the second part of the chapter we will contextualize the New Testament in the historic world of its day.

What is history?

Can a person trust the historical veracity of the New Testament? As with the veracity of all historical sources the question of the New Testament's reliability is complex. It will help to appreciate the complexity by spending some time with the question: What is history?

We may begin with a simple definition. History, someone has written, is a story about the past that is both significant and true. The definition implies that history is not synonymous with the past. The past is immense and unrecoverable. The historian's reconstruction of the past is always partial. The historian's knowledge of the past depends upon the available evidence and the available evidence is always partial.

To further complicate the question of historical truth we must also acknowledge that historians write their story of the past from a particular point of view. Likewise consumers of history read the historian's account of the past from a particular point of view. In other words, reconstructions of the past are comprised of two elements—facts and the interpretation of their significance. The same evidence looked at from different points of view appears differently. Is one point of view truer than another? It depends on your vantage point.

None of this suggests that history is arbitrary. Historical reconstructions operate within certain constraints. If historians expect readers to regard their account as credible they must operate within the constraints of the available evidence. As well, histories are written and read in communities. The different interests, represented throughout the community, militate on the basis of the culture's standard of truth against the tendency to falsify. We work out the significance and the truth of the past together. The process of historical reconstruction ever continues; we never finish.

Given these realities three considerations promise to make our inquiry into the past fruitful: 1) Self-awareness about the point of view from which the story of the past is written and read. 2) Sources from which the story of the past is constructed. 3) Criteria by which to judge the significance and truth of proposed stories of the past.

1) The Place of Self-Awareness in Writing and Reading the Story of the Past

On the basis of what we have said previously about the importance and centrality of point of view, self-awareness would seem a good beginning point in the enterprise of historical understanding. Self-awareness about what shapes and informs the point of view from which we see the past and its significance is crucial. The question of self-awareness may be framed by a series of sub-questions: What basis do I have for offering a reconstruction of the past? What basis do I have for accepting or rejecting a particular reconstruction of the past? What vested interests do I have to protect? Why does this story of the past matter to me? From what point of view do I look into the past? What has and continues to shape my point of view?

2) The Question of Sources

The second consideration concerns how we regard the available evidence from which to construct the story of the past. Several common-place distinctions made by professional historians will prove helpful to our study of the New Testament's historical veracity. In the reconstruction of the past historians distinguish between two kinds of sources: **primary sources** and **secondary works**. Historians define primary sources as documents produced in proximity to the era under investigation. No other artifact lies behind them. Secondary sources, removed from the actual events, attempt to truthfully synthesize the significance of past events. Let's take a closer look at the significance of these distinctions for historical understanding related to the question of available sources.

Primary Sources

Primary sources, we have said, are materials that date from the historical era under investigation. They may be divided into two categories—**voluntary** and **involuntary**. **Voluntary Sources** are self-conscious historical accounts written by event participants or observers for posterity. General Grant's memoirs, if there is such a source, would be a voluntary primary source from which to reconstruct a history of the civil war era. **Involuntary Sources** emerge from documents of the era that were written to address persons and circumstances immediately within the era. Abraham Lincoln's Gettysburg Address would be an example of a primary, involuntary source.

With respect to the New Testament writings one might consider Luke's two-part contribution to the corpus—The Gospel According to St. Luke and Acts of Apostles—as an example of self-conscious history of Christian origins (so, a voluntary source). In these works Luke quite self-consciously seeks to tell the story of how the church emerged out of and was shaped by the encounter with Jesus. In the opening verses of his Gospel Luke explains his purpose and how he has executed it: "After investigating everything carefully . . . I decided to write an orderly account . . . so that you may know the truth concerning the things about which you have been instructed" (Luke 1:3–4). The Greek word which stands behind the English term, "orderly account," in fact means history as the craft was understood in Luke's day. This is not to say that Luke was writing the story of Jesus and the early church from a neutral, unbiased point of view. Neither Luke's story nor any other story comes down to us without bias. The story of the past is always told from one point of view or another. In fact, point of view is essential to bringing out the significance of what is being told. Luke's point of view is that to understand the full significance of the reported events they must be viewed as acts of God (Luke 24:44–49; Acts 1:8).

Paul's First Letter to the Corinthians would be an example of an involuntary source. In the letter Paul addresses troubling rumors and questions about which the congregation has sought his counsel (see 1 Cor. 1:11 and 7:1, for example). Paul writes not as a historian for posterity. As an apostle he writes out of pastoral concern to and for a community of faith contemporary to his time.

Both types of primary sources—voluntary and involuntary—prove equally indispensable to telling the story of the past. One is not more truthful than the other, just different. They must be regarded for what they are. Just as the question of self-awareness could be broken down into a series of sub-questions so also the question of primary and secondary sources can be broken down into a series of sub-questions that help to see them for what they are. What is the literary nature of the document? Why was the particular document written? By whom was it written? For whom was it written? What is the purpose of the writing? How is it related to other documents of the era?

Secondary Sources

Written by historians removed from the actual events, secondary works attempt to synthesize the significance and truth of what occurred in the era under investigation. *The American Civil War: A Military History* by John Keegan would be an example of a secondary work on the civil war era. With respect to the New Testament *The History of Primitive Christianity* by Hans Conzelmann would be an example of a Secondary Source. Students of history find Secondary Sources important and useful to our historical understanding for a variety of reasons. They provide from a point of view, and usually for a particular purpose, a synthesized story of the past. They help us understand how the past has shaped our world. They help us navigate the political, economic, and social dimensions of contemporary life. They instill values and cultivate solidarity. As with primary sources, critical reception of secondary accounts involves a series of similar sub-questions: What is the point of view of the secondary source? For whom has it been written? Why has it been written? What primary and secondary sources have been employed in its reconstruction of the past? How have these sources been employed and to what end?

3) Criteria by which to Judge Significant and True

The third consideration related to historical understanding concerns the standard by which we judge a story of the past to be true. Ultimately, as we acknowledged at the outset, historical inquiry seeks to establish whether the reported events of the narrative actually occurred in "real time." Are they true? For the reasons that we have previously set forth it should now be apparent that with respect to the past, an absolute, complete, definitive, final picture is never available to us in the present. Does it mean that we can never have confidence in our picture of the past? Does it mean that we can never consider the contemporary significance of what took place in the past? Donald Juel has suggested, given the kinds of answers that historical investigation yields, that an appropriate standard of historical credibility would be: "Can a reasonable person look at the facts and take them seriously?"[1] That standard of evidence seems to me sufficient for our purposes. By that standard we may view the text of the New Testament as a window through which to consider the contemporary significance of the reported events.

Historical Investigation and the New Testament

The literature of the New Testament was written around 2000 years ago in a cultural world very different from our world. Therefore, intelligent and respectful interpretation will be sensitive to issues surrounding the historical distance between the contemporary reader and the ancient text. Critical issues include: language; culture; patterns of thought; symbols, traditions, and events; political, social, and economic conditions of the era; and so forth.

Such historical inquiry into the New Testament era (0–150 CE) consists of sifting through ancient documents. In the case of the New Testament era the documentation that provides our sources includes both canonical materials, for example, Mark's Gospel, as well as non-canonical works, for example, Josephus's *Antiquities of the Jews*. Appreciation of the historical context of the New Testament writings will be helped by

---

[1]"Your Word is Truth," in *Shaping the Scriptural Imagination: Truth and Meaning, and the Theological Interpretation of the Bible.* Edited by Shane Berg and Matthew L Skinner (Waco: Baylor University Press, 2011), 19.

the attempt to track down allusions to persons, places, times, social and political circumstances, customs, and beliefs not automatically known to modern readers. By such means of inquiry modern readers can reconstruct the "world" of the New Testament.

Actually, Paul Ricoeur, an influential philosopher and literary critic of the twentieth century, has suggested that it is helpful to think of **"Three Worlds"** when reading literature from the past—the world **behind** the text, the world **of** the text, and the world **in front of** the text. This distinction is in fact useful for structuring historical inquiry.

The World of the Text

Inquiry into **The World of the Text** focuses attention on what takes place in the narrative world which the author has constructed. At this level of inquiry, using the tools and insights of **Narrative Analysis**, interpretation seeks to make evident the portrait of Jesus as a character in a narrative. In this aspect of interpretation the question—"Is it true?"—has to do with the way in which the narrative unfolds. For example: Is it true that Jesus was crucified as a messianic pretender? As a literary question, a question of what transpired in the "world of the narrative," the answer can be determined on the basis of literary inquiry into the data provided by the text. We can say definitively, for example, that within the narrative world constructed by Mark, Jesus was executed as a messianic pretender. The data of the text supports the conclusion: "The inscription of the charge against him read, 'The King of the Jews'" (Mark 15:26). The soldiers mocked him as "King of the Jews" (Mark 15:17ff).

How this "fact" of what has occurred within the narrative world constructed by Mark relates to the "fact" of what has occurred in the world of real time is another question. It is a question of history, in Ricoeur's terminology, a question of what has occurred in the "World Behind the Text."

World Behind the Text

The **World Behind the Text** refers to the events which have occurred previous to the writing and to which the writing bears witness. For example, the Gospels of the New Testament attest that Jesus was executed as a false Messiah and was raised from the dead on the third day. Historical inquiry seeks to establish whether this event of the narrative occurred in "real time." Is it true? As Donald Juel has suggested, given the kinds of answers that historical investigation yields, an appropriate answer would be: "Can a reasonable person look at the evidence for Jesus's death and resurrection from the dead and take it seriously?"

Together our task is to sift through the available evidence in conversation with one another as we seek to piece together the significance and truth of what transpired in the New Testament era. The sophisticated inquirer appreciates that **history** is always more than facts. It is **facts** put together **with interpretation** of their significance for life in the here and now, or as Ricoeur says, for life in the world in front of the text.

The World In Front of the Text

With respect to the **World In Front of the Text**, interpretation focuses on the experience of readers as they encounter the story and message of the New Testament. Of course reading the New Testament has a two thousand year history. Thus inquiry can focus on the reported experience of past readers, which may be instructive in the sense that contemporary readings of the text tend to be filtered through the earlier experience of past readers.

Ultimately, interpretation is interested in what happens to contemporary readers in the encounter with the text. In this regard inquiry will seek to determine the rhetorical strategies and conventions employed by the writer to bring about the experience of the reader. Why, for example, do readers tend to side with the disciples of Jesus and against the Jewish and Greco-Roman detractors of Jesus? Part of the answer may lie in the fact that readers share the sympathetic prejudice of the text toward Christians. The question however is whether the text itself shapes the experience of readers in such a way as to reinforce or cultivate sympathetic prejudice toward the Christian faith. Rhetorical inquiry seeks to understand how the text cultivates this prejudice in its readers.

With respect to the experience of readers, the question—"Is it true?"—has a somewhat different connotation than it does when inquiry focuses on the question of the historical or literary integrity of the text. At this point, inquiry seeks to determine whether the claims of the text are theologically true and reliable. Does the New Testament tell the way it is with God and life in relation to him? Is it true, for instance, that Jesus is the Savior of the World? If so, in what sense is he the Savior? What does he save humanity from and for? What is the implication for the faith and life of contemporary people?

The Jesus of History, Fact and Significance

Can a reasonable person look at the evidence and find the claim of Jesus's historical existence plausible? Most historians answer, yes. What to make of his significance for faith and life is another question. It is the central question of the earliest Christian sources on Jesus. The writings of the New Testament are not so much taken up with proving that Jesus actually existed as a historical person. They presume that it may be taken for granted. Their aim is to bring out the significance of Jesus for the faith and life of their contemporary readers. Sensitive readers of today, with a careful eye turned toward reading the New Testament in historical context, will appreciate the fact of it.

Historical Context of the New Testament Era[2]

The New Testament tells the story of Jesus and his significance for faith, with special focus on the central questions of theology—Who is God? What does it mean to be

---

[2]See Appendix C for a timeline of the relevant history.

human? The telling of the story is informed and shaped by the institutions, traditions, symbols, and rationality of Jewish and Greco-Roman cultures of first-century Palestine. The encounter with the Jesus of the New Testament by readers of today will be enriched in proportion to their knowledge and understanding of the Greco-Roman world of the first century. This is the world behind the New Testament.

Actually, it would be more accurate to say that there are really two worlds behind the New Testament. There is the world of the historical Jesus and there is the world of the **evangelists**.[3] Frequently scholars refer to the era of the evangelists as the apostolic age, roughly synonymous with the period of time during which the New Testament was written (50–110 CE). We may assume the conventional dates for the historical Jesus, to be roughly 0–33 CE. Our earliest primary sources are the letters of Paul, generally assumed to be written during the 50s of the Common Era. Historians normally date the composition of the Gospels of the New Testament between 70 and 100 CE. In the forty or so years between the historical Jesus and the production of the Gospels there were significant developments that affected the way in which the Gospel writers told the story. For our purposes the three most significant developments were: 1) the destruction of the Temple (70 CE), 2) the expulsion of Christians from the Jewish synagogue (by 100 CE), and 3) the eventual Gentile dominance in the constituency of the Christian community (by 100 CE). Let's take a closer look at these developments in their historical context.

Beginnings: Christianity and Rabbinic Judaism

Initially the Christian movement began not as a new religion, but as a relatively small **sectarian** movement within the Jewish community. These Jews believed that Jesus fulfilled the prophecy of God's promised **Messiah**. Early Jewish Christians articulated their faith primarily in the language, traditions, and symbols of the Jewish Scriptures. Gradually, the movement expanded beyond its Jewish borders into the **Gentile**[4] community. Both of these developments—the claim that Jesus was the long-awaited Messiah and fellowship with Gentiles—provoked bitter and deep conflict with the larger Jewish community. Although the details are unclear, by the end of the first century CE the followers of Jesus were excommunicated from the **synagogue**.[5] As well, by this time Gentile members outnumbered Jewish members within the community. From this time forward the followers of Jesus began to identify themselves as Christian. The term derives from the Greek translation of the Hebrew Messiah. Increasingly the Christian message was articulated according to Greek conceptualities.

In general the New Testament writings were penned prior to the separation of the Christian believers from the Jewish community. Thus, in the New Testament the question of what it means to be Christian remains entangled with the question of what it means to be Jewish in the Greco-Roman world of the first century. In fact the Jewish

---

[3]Evangelist is the term generally used to reference the New Testament writers who committed the story of Jesus to paper.

[4]Gentile is a Jewish term to designate non-Jews. The term is inclusive of, but does not distinguish between, the different ethnic and cultural groups that comprise the populations of the ancient near-east: Egyptians, Syrians, Romans, Greeks, and so forth.

[5]Synagogue designates the local assembly of Jews, gathered for worship, study, and fellowship.

scholar, Alan Segal, argues that after the destruction of the Temple in 70 CE working out what it means to be Christian was one way to answer the question of what it means to be Jewish. The other tenable answer to the question was offered by the Jewish sect known in the New Testament and other sources of the era as the **Pharisees**. This sect is best understood as a lay-renewal movement. The Pharisees believed that the law of God as made known in the Ten Commandments provides the basis of living in relation to God and the neighbor. For the Pharisees the questions—Who is God? What does it mean to be human? —were answered in the Ten Commandments. They sought to extend the teaching of the Ten Commandments to cover every eventuality of daily life. Toward this end they developed a teaching method to make explicitly evident what it means to observe God's law in the rough and tumble of everyday life. Eventually the Pharisee party developed into modern-day Rabbinic Judaism.

Thus, these two religions—Christianity and Rabbinic Judaism—trace their origins to the same era. The followers of Jesus and the Pharisees vied against one another to establish which faction of the Jewish community was the true heir to the faith tradition represented in the Jewish Scriptures. Our purpose in this portion of the chapter is to put the conflict between the followers of Jesus and the Pharisees in historic perspective.

At the time of Jesus Jews had lived under the domination of **Hellenism**[6] for three centuries. The ambition of Alexander the Great (d. 323 BCE) had been to take the world captive to Greek ways. His ambition met with remarkable success. Of course not all Jews were eager to accept the Greek ways. Some in fact resisted fiercely. But even Jews who sought to maintain their identity as defined in the history of Israel and preserved in the Jewish Scriptures, in the end found it impossible to resist Greek ways. By the time of the New Testament era (50–110 CE) it had been necessary to translate the Jewish Scriptures into Greek, so thoroughly had Greek replaced Hebrew as the spoken language among Jews.

The history of both traditions reads most clearly through the lens of God's promises to the ancient Israel. The followers of Jesus believed that, as the promised Messiah, Jesus would establish the everlasting rule of God's love over creation. As God had promised David, "I will not take [away] . . . my steadfast love . . . Your house and your kingdom shall be made sure forever before me" (2 Sam. 7:15–16). The Pharisees on the other hand believed that the future of creation depended on promises of God associated with the **Torah**. As God had promised Joshua at the time when the people were about to take possession of their homeland, "This book of the law shall not depart out of your mouth; you shall meditate on it day and night, so that you may be careful to act in accordance with all that is written in it. For then you shall make your way prosperous, and then you shall be successful" (Jos. 1:8).

There was very little in the experience of the Jewish community during the first century that would have offered assurance that God was keeping his promise, whether the

---

[6]Hellenism refers to the influence of Greek ways of thinking and living. Historians date the era of Hellenistic domination from the death of Alexander in 323 BCE to the establishment of the Roman Empire in 198 BCE. But even after the Romans succeeded the descendants of Alexander politically, the influence of Greek ways of thinking and living continued to dominate the human imagination.

promise of the Messiah or the promise of the Torah. In just about every way imaginable Jews of the first century, especially after the destruction of the Temple, were in crisis. Not only did they suffer political uncertainty in relation to Roman rule, the most recent occupational ruler of Palestine, but they suffered religious uncertainty that went right to the heart of their self-understanding as the people of Yahweh. Simply put, the crisis could be understood in the question: If we are the favored people of God then why do we suffer such overwhelming misfortune and adversity? The crisis of that question had been in the making for centuries.

The Long Slide toward Disaster

The political fortunes of Israel as the elect people of God had been in steady and deep decline ever since the glory days of King David and Solomon in the tenth century BCE.[7] The year 587 BCE marked a catastrophic watershed in the declining fortunes. In that year Babylon, the reigning superpower, attacked and destroyed Jerusalem, including the Temple, and forced the leading citizens of Israel into exile. Eventually, in 516 BCE, the Temple was rebuilt, but never again did the people of Israel possess their homeland by self-rule. Their land was occupied by one superpower after another—Babylon, Persia, Greece, Rome. A brief sketch of the political and military lay of Palestine during the so-called Second Temple period of Jewish history[8] tells the story of the religious crisis in which Christianity and Rabbinic Judaism arose.

After the death of Alexander (323 BCE) Greek rule of Palestine was divided between two dynasties, the Macedonian Ptolemies and the Syrian Seleucids. The Ptolemies exercised relaxed control, permitting Jews a measure of self-determination, politically and religiously. Jews however did not fare so well under the Seleucids. Taxes were increased; persecutions were executed. Whether under the relaxed rule of the Ptolemies or the oppressive rule of the Seleucids, Hellenism continued to make inroads into Jewish life. Jews were deeply divided over what concessions could be made to the Greek ways without compromising their identity as the people of God. Eventually the conflict broke out in civil war. The Syrian Seleucids responded by imposing harsher measures than ever. In effect they outlawed the practice of the Jewish religion. Torah scrolls were burned. Circumcision, the external sign of belonging to the Jewish people, was punishable by death. It was unlawful for Jews even to visit the Temple precincts. Yahweh was evicted from the Temple and it was rededicated to the worship of Zeus. These were among the darkest times ever in the history of Israel. The Book of Daniel, probably written during this time, reflects the desperation that many Jews suffered during their fiery ordeal. It also reflects that Jews did not lose hope that God would eventually send the Messiah to rescue the people and restore their fortunes as the people of God.

---

[7]Consult the Historical Time Line to see the big picture of people, events, and writings of the New Testament era and the events leading up to it. See Appendix C.

[8]There are many good secondary works that focus on this period of history. Students will find helpful from the Jewish perspective: Jacob Neusner. *Judaism in the Beginning of Christianity* (Minneapolis: Fortress Press, 1984) and Shaye Cohen. *From the Maccabees to the Mishnah*. Second Edition (Louisville: Westminster John Knox Press, 2006). Both are concise and very readable.

According to the hope that God had not abandoned them Jews did not take their oppression passively. In the second century BCE, under the leadership of Judas Maccabeus and his sons, the Jews successfully revolted. They managed to reinstitute self-rule and reconsecrated the Temple to the worship of Yahweh. The Hasmonean Dynasty—as the rulers descended from the Maccabees were known—was, however, troubled with eternal strife throughout its hundred year rule. Eventually in an attempt to secure their rule against one another two rival brothers of the family appealed independently of one another for help from Rome. Rome was only too happy to intervene. In 63 BCE Palestine became a vassal of Rome, first under Pompey and then under Julius Caesar. For services rendered, Caesar appointed the Idumean, Antipater, to rule over Palestine. By decree of Caesar Augustus, Antipater's son inherited rule of Palestine and is the Roman puppet ruling Galilee at the time of Jesus's birth.

The Crisis of the Temple's Destruction

Herod was an able, if ruthless, ruler. To eliminate prospective rivals to the throne he killed members of his own family, including his wife and sons. Although there is no corroboration outside of the New Testament, Matthew attests that for the same reason Herod responded to the rumors of a child born to be king by dispatching his troops to slaughter all children two years old and younger. Certain quasi-religio-political parties, like the aristocratic Herodians and the Sadducees

© 2012 JupiterImages Corp.

may have ridden the coattails of Herod's power but it is not likely that even they shed many tears when he himself died in 4 BCE.

After his death the Romans divided the rule of Palestine among three surviving sons of Herod. They were all as ruthless as their father but not nearly as able rulers as their father had been. In response to their failed rule Palestine was subjected to the direct rule of Rome. Readers of the New Testament are familiar with at least a couple of the Roman governors. Quirinius, according to Luke, was governor of Syria when Jesus was born. Pilate was governor of Judea when Jesus was executed. Whether under the puppet kings or direct occupation the people of Palestine resented Roman rule. From time to time guerilla movements—sometimes fomented of messianic ambition—mounted rebellions against Rome, but always with same disastrous results. Two wars in particular (66–70 CE and 132–135 CE) led to the destruction of Jerusalem, including the Temple, and the disbursement of Jews from Palestine.

The period of Second Temple Judaism begins in 515 BCE some years after the Persian King, Cyrus, allowed exiled Jews to return to Palestine (538 BCE). High on the agenda of the returning exiles was the rebuilding of the Temple. Construction continued under wave after wave of renovation down to the massive restoration project of Herod in 20 BCE. The fact that the people of Israel believed that God had chosen this place as his earthly residence explains the enormous devotion of resources to the reconstruction of the Temple. While it existed Jewish life revolved around Temple. Along with Torah, the Temple symbolized the special relationship that Israel had with God.

Imagine the crisis created by its destruction in 70 CE. Why would God allow the destruction of the Temple? What did it mean for Israel in relation to God? During the formative period of Rabbinic Judaism and Christianity these questions met with different explanations. The **Sadducees**, for example, were a small aristocratic group based in Jerusalem. Their political power was anchored in the Temple and depended upon the good graces of Rome. One can well imagine that they argued that Israel's ill-fortunes were due to the fact that God had sent Rome in much the same manner that he once upon a time had sent Cyrus to unite and give a future to Palestine. By refusing to accept and cooperate with the divinely appointed Roman rule the Jewish people brought the judgment of God upon themselves in the form of destruction and exile.

Zealots might have argued one hundred and eighty degrees the reverse. The Zealots were a revolutionary movement which believed and taught that it was more holy to spill the blood of a Roman than to offer sacrifices on the altar in the Temple. The outlook of the Zealots was similar to that of the Maccabees. In their day the Maccabees were willing to sacrifice everything to fight for the cause of God. The Zealots were critical of their contemporaries because unlike the Maccabees, present-day Jews, like the Sadducees, refused to take up arms against the Roman enemies of God. They thus brought upon themselves the judgment of God.

The **Pharisees**, on the other hand, would have argued that both the Sadducees and the Zealots were wrong in their analysis of Israel's misfortunes. Given their allegiance and dedication to Torah, the Pharisees might have argued that it was the failure of the larger community to observe the statutes of Torah in daily life that had brought the judgment of God.

"**Jewish Christians**" would have found the explanations of all three sects—Sadducees, Zealots and Pharisees—to be off the mark. Their explanation of Israel's fortunes would most certainly have centered on Israel's failure to embrace Jesus as the long-awaited Messiah. They might well have reasoned that in Jesus God had sent his saving Messiah. Popular rejection, especially among leaders who should have known better, had brought the judgment of God.

Of course after the two disastrous Jewish wars (66–70 CE and 132–135 CE) resulting in the destruction of the Temple and the exile of Jews from what was left of Jerusalem the only tenable explanation to the troubles of Israel was that offered by Jewish Christians, on the one hand, and that offered by the Pharisees, on the other hand. The New Testament tells the Christian story. The Talmud tells the story of Rabbinic Judaism. The Christian story we take up in our study of the New Testament. In conclusion to this section a brief word about the development of Rabbinic Judaism.

The Story of Rabbinic Judaism

The story of how the Pharisee movement developed into Rabbinic Judaism continues through the exiled community of legal scholars under the leadership of Johanan ben Zakkai. Following the destruction of Jerusalem the group had relocated in the town of Jamnia. To this group Rome granted permission to rule the religious and civic life of Palestinian Jews. Over the course of the next three centuries the identity and life of the Jewish community was heavily influenced by the outlook of these teachers of Torah. The story of the spreading influence is impossible to tell because historians lack source materials from the period. What is known is that by the fourth century these legal scholars had produced a significant corpus of literature, consisting of the **Midrashim** (commentaries on Tanakh), **Mishnah** (laws listed according to subject governed), and the **Gemara** (commentary on the Mishnah). Together the Mishnah and the Gemara form the **Talmud**, which roughly speaking serves Rabbinic Judaism in the same way that the New Testament serves the Christian community. Thus by the fourth century Judaism has become a religion of the book and Jewish life has become Torah observance.

The animosity between Christians and Pharisees in the New Testament is no doubt attributable to the tension between these two Jewish sects as they vied for the future of Israel and sought to establish themselves one against the other as the rightful heir to the tradition of Israel as it was set forth in Tanakh. As Alan Segal explains, "Like Jacob and Esau, the twin sons of Isaac and Rebecca, the two religions fought in the womb. Throughout their youth they followed very different paths, quarreling frequently about their father's blessing. As was the case with Rebecca's children, the conflict between Judaism and Christianity molded their characters and determined their destinies."[9] Neither religion can adequately be understood apart from the history of their origins. To take up the New Testament into theological discourse today necessarily involves the student in the study of history.

Historical Inquiry—Work Sheet

Developing facility with historical method, like any discipline taught in the university, is a life-long project. The tips indicated below suggest ways to conduct, responsibly and fruitfully, historical investigation into the world of Jesus and the world of the early church. Regarding the New Testament text as a source for reconstructing these two eras, students will find it helpful to proceed by:

1. List Persons, Places, Customs, Imagery, Traditions, and any other references in the text with which you are unfamiliar, for which additional historical background seems to be required in order to more fully understand the reference.

---

[9] Alan Segal, *Rebecca's Children: Judaism and Christianity in the Roman World* (Cambridge: Harvard University Press, 1986), 1.

2. There are two ways to develop background information on references in the text.

   a) Read the New Testament text for the purpose of finding information that helps to broaden understanding of historical reference, especially as the notes direct attention to material from the Jewish Scriptures (Christian Old Testament).

   b) Consult an Encyclopedia of the Bible or other resource to develop a background sketch of the references you have identified in the text.

3. Helpful References include:

   • *The New Interpreter's Dictionary of the Bible.* 5 volumes. Ed. by Katherine Sakenfeld. Nashville: Abingdon Press, 2006–2010. Contains short, up-to-date articles by scholarly contributors on the writings, themes, characters, places, customs, and other matters related to interpreting the Bible.

   • *Oxford Bible Atlas.* Second Edition. Ed. by Adrian Curtis. London: Oxford University Press, 2009. Contains pictures, articles, maps, and charts detailing many of the geo-political matters related to the study of the New Testament.

   • *The Oxford Bible Commentary.* Ed. by John Barton and John Muddiman. Oxford: Oxford University Press, 2001. Contains introductory articles to each of the biblical writings by respected scholars.

   • Early Christian Writings: http://www.earlychristianwritings.com/

   • The Catholic Encyclopedia: http://www.newadvent.org/cathen/

Terms:

Evangelist	Hellenism
Apostolic Age	Torah / Law
Sect / Sectarian Movement	Midrashim
Messiah	Mishnah
Gentile	Gemara
Synagogue	Talmud
Pharisees	

Secondary Sources for Further Study of the New Testament Era:

Everett Ferguson. *Backgrounds of Early Christianity (Second Edition).* Grand Rapids: Eerdmans Publishing Company, 1993. Fleshes out the political, cultural, and intellectual world in which Christianity originated.

Maxwell Miller. *The Old Testament and the Historian.* Philadelphia: Fortress, 1976. Explains how historians use the available evidence to make judgments about the historical reliability of the Old Testament materials.

Bo Reicke. *The New Testament Era: The World of the Bible from 500 B.C. to A.D. 100.* Translated by David Green. Philadelphia: Fortress Press, 1968. Fleshes out the political, cultural, and intellectual world in which Christianity originated.

Calvin J. Roetzel. *The World That Shaped the New Testament, Revised Edition.* Louisville: Westminster John Knox Press, 2002. Fleshes out the political, cultural, and intellectual world in which Christianity originated.

Alan Segal. *Rebecca's Children: Judaism and Christianity in the Roman World.* Cambridge: Harvard Press, 1986. Segal argues that Judaism and Christianity, as rivals, developed in the same historical context. The two traditions represent dramatically different views of the Jewish Scriptures, in part due to their vantage point. Judaism viewed Torah as the definitive revelation of God whereas Christianity saw Jesus in that light.

Robert Louis Wilken. *The Christians as the Romans Saw Them, Second Edition.* New Haven: Yale University Press, 2003. Fleshes out the political, cultural, and intellectual world in which Christianity originated. Special attention is given to the way in which the Christian movement and Christians might have appeared in light of the emperor cult.

Study Questions:

1. Define history.

2. What is the distinction between the past and history?

3. How does "point of view" affect the view of the past?

4. How does Paul Ricoeur's Three Worlds of the Text help students to focus on the text as a window on the past?

5. Explain the distinction between primary and secondary sources as well as between voluntary and involuntary sources.

6. What historical questions are of most interest to you with respect to the New Testament?

7. What are the criteria by which we determine whether our historical reconstruction has been successful in constructing a reliable and usable history?

8. Case Study: Did Jesus of Nazareth exist in real time? On what considerations do you base your answer?

Chapter 5

The New Testament as Rhetorical Speech

Readers frequently approach the New Testament expecting to find information. Whether they are looking for historical information about the origins of Christian faith, theological information about the Christian view of God, or information about Christian morality, the expectation is not disappointed. The New Testament contains historical information about Jesus and his disciples, about Christian origins and beliefs, about the fortunes and ill-fortunes of Jesus's followers within the Jewish community and the greater Greco-Roman world of the first century. As well, the New Testament contains information about how Christians are to live in relation to God, others, and creation. Readers however do not fully appreciate the New Testament if they view it only as a source of information. As biblical scholars, like Donald Juel and Robert Fowler, have shown the literature of the New Testament works to move its readers in relation to God.[1] This is to say that the literature of the New Testament functions, like language in general, not only as a container of meaning but also as a dynamic that provokes response and, in fact, creates new realities. As the narrator of Mark's story sums up the significance of Jesus, "The kingdom of God has drawn near, repent and believe the good news" (Mark 1:14).

We are sufficiently familiar with language in its symbolic capacity to name persons, places, and things that it requires no further explanation. Likewise, language in its conceptual capacity to tell the meaning of things and ideas requires little explanation. By the time students enter the university they have had plenty of experience exploring conceptual realties like courage, justice, and love. However, for the sake of reading the New Testament it is worthwhile to consider how language functions in its dynamic capacity to create new realities and move audiences to new thoughts and actions. Think, for example, of the great orators of the twentieth century. The oratory of Martin Luther King Jr., for example, mobilized people to non-violently resist unjust racial laws during the 1960s. The movement led to the extension of American juridical ideals to all of her citizens, regardless of race. The word proved mightier than the sword.

Martin Luther King, Jr.
January 15, 1929

© 2012 JupiterImages Corp.

[1]See, for example, Donald Juel's *The Gospel of Mark* (Nashville: Abingdon Press, 1999) and Robert Fowler's *Let the Reader Understand: Reader-Response Criticism and the Gospel of Mark* (Minneapolis: Fortress Press, 1991).

Language may be used to include or exclude, to hurt or heal, to inspire or frighten, to endear and to repulse, and so forth. Perhaps promise-making best exemplifies language in its dynamic capacity. When two people make the promise of marriage—to love and to cherish, for richer, for poorer, in sickness and in health—it changes their situation. They are no longer two, but one. The New Testament, as Word of God, functions in just this way, as a dynamic that has the capacity to change the human situation.

The New Testament as the Word of God

The Apostle Paul in fact characterizes the central message of the New Testament as "the power of God for salvation" (Rom. 1:16). Paul writes not only to inform but to shape and move the readers of his letters by proclaiming to and for them the saving good news of Jesus. For example, throughout the brief, but potent, Letter to the Galatians Paul argues against alternative views for a particular understanding of the gospel of Jesus and its implication for how the community lives. Toward the end of the letter he draws together the proclamation of the gospel and its implication for life, "For freedom Christ has set us free. Stand firm, therefore, and do not submit again to a yoke of slavery" (5:1). The passage raises many questions: In what sense did the Galatians suffer under "a yoke of slavery"? Is there a sense in which suffering under "a yoke of slavery" is also true of the human condition universally, today as well as then? How has Christ set free the Galatian Christians? For what have the Galatian Christians been set free? What if anything does the talk of slavery and freedom have to do with us today? We are not prepared to take up these questions at this stage of our introduction. Our point is that Paul regards the gospel, Word of Christ, as a power which moves people into a new reality, liberates from what holds them bound and captive; liberates them, free to be. In fact, as Paul makes clear in his Letter to the Romans, the transformation that occurs in the life of the believer is nothing short of a death and resurrection (see Rom. 6:7ff.).

On the basis of the gospel and in light of the Galatian situation Paul, throughout the letter, declares that the letter's recipients are in fact justified to live in the freedom of their new situation; they need not bow again to the old life in which they were compelled to prove themselves worthy of belonging to the "in-crowd." Paul draws out the implication of his proclamation along the ordinary path of the standard rhetorical conventions and strategies current in the Greco-Roman world of his day. How else, humanly speaking, could he have expected to move the Galatian Christians to his point of view? Theological argument, like argument in any other discipline, is subject to the current ways of reasoning. Whether the logic of Paul's proclamation will continue to engage and move people today cannot be determined ahead of time. A rhetorical approach can however recover Paul's argument so that it may be made again in the context of contemporary life. And then we have to see how it will affect hearers today.

The narrative material of the New Testament works in the same way as Paul's letters. The Gospels, Acts of the Apostles, and Revelation work to shape the thinking of readers in relation to God and to move them to live in ways fitting to God's action in Christ. Luke, for example, acknowledges that he has undertaken to tell the story of Jesus and the church in order that his audience may "know the truth" concerning the things about which it has been instructed (Luke 1:4). Similarly, John declares that he has written the story of Jesus that his audience may be moved "to believe that Jesus is the Messiah, the Son of God, and that through believing . . . may have life in his name" (John 20:30–31). In the course of executing their rhetorical objectives the narrative authors of the New Testament have adopted and adapted the story telling ways of their day. In this chapter we explore the ways in which the New Testament literature works to create, shape, and move its readers. Again, to emphasize what we have been saying in the previous chapters, our aim is not merely to study the writings of the New Testament, but to study them for the sake of the contemporary reader's encounter and engagement, so that the writings may have the same effect on readers today as in the past.

A Rhetorical Approach

In scholarly discourse the art of using language to affect or move an audience is referred to as **rhetoric**. A rhetorical approach to the study of the New Testament seeks to understand how the writings, and their interpretation, work to shape and move readers. The power of the New Testament to shape and move readers is not exhausted by the rhetorical skill of its authors. The Christian tradition claims that the works of the Bible as they are taken up into the life of the church are the means by which God creates and sustains the life of faith. We do not adequately appreciate the power of the New Testament to shape and move us until we consider the New Testament as the Word of God, the living voice of God. In this chapter our focus is on the "means" by which God speaks. We focus on the rhetorical conventions and strategies employed by the New Testament writings to move readers to believe, understand, and live by trust in the promise of God. In the biblical view, trusting God's promise defines what it means to live by faith (Rom. 3:21–26).

The Aim of a Rhetorical Approach

A rhetorical approach aims to help contemporary readers appreciate the conventions and strategies employed by the New Testament authors so that the full force of the writings may be experienced anew in the twenty-first century. Biblical interpretation from a rhetorical point of view may be compared to the study of a theatrical script. The study of a theatrical script is not an end in itself. Plays are written to be performed. Think for example of Shakespeare's *Macbeth*. A contemporary performance of the play will involve the study of sixteenth-century English life, language, politics, theater, and so forth. Actors and directors seek to expand their background knowledge and understanding through study in order to present a faithful and effective performance of the drama. Audiences study in order to better appreciate the performance of the drama. Neither for actors nor for audiences is study an end in itself. Of interest is what happens when the drama comes to life on the stage. The same applies to the interpretation of the Bible. Interpretation seeks to present a faithful and affective "reading" of the New Testament to contemporary audiences so that they may experience the rhetorical force of the material. Understanding the rhetoric of the New Testament and its interpretation is complex. Over the centuries, students keen to understand the art of using language to shape and move an audience have found the insights of Aristotle helpful. His insights focus and order rhetorical inquiry of the New Testament.

Aristotle's Contribution

Aristotle observed that there are three characters involved in any act of communication—the character of the speaker (ethos), the character of the speech (logos), and the character of the audience (pathos).[2] Aristotle perhaps took for granted the obvious importance of context. For that reason it may have gone without saying in his discussion of communication. But for our purposes it is worth pointing out that in some measure at least context determines how the words of speakers are heard. Therefore interpretation of the New Testament must take into account the context of the readers and hearers. Scholarly study of the New Testament has often been chiefly interested to understand what the writings meant to the original readers in the ancient context. As we acknowledged in the chapter on the New Testament as history we too are interested in that aspect of things, but only in so far as it serves a faithful and effective reading of the New Testament in the contemporary context of life today. The New Testament is not merely an artifact from antiquity, a literature for another people in another place, at another time. It is the Scripture of the Christian community, past and present. Readers of the Bible have discovered that whatever historical changes have occurred in the political, social, and economic context of human life, in the theological context people of today have much in common with the people of the Bible. The Word of God promises to do to us today what it has done to countless generations all the way back to the generation of the Bible. Our interest is to hear the literature in its own voice. Or, perhaps better—as Aristotle has taught us—we seek to imagine ourselves in the rhetorical triangle created by the interaction between the three characters of the New Testament text—speaker, audience, and speech.

The Rhetorical Triangle

The so-called rhetorical triangle pictures the implication of Aristotle's insight for reading the New Testament. Taking its cue from Aristotle's insight a rhetorical approach seeks to illuminate what happens, and what should happen, on the basis of the "speech" between "speaker" and "audience," as readers engage the writings of the New Testament.

---

[2]Aristotle. *Poetics.* Loeb Classical Library (Cambridge: Harvard University Press, 1927).

By Whom: Writer / Speaker

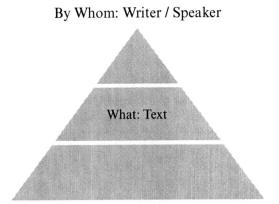

What: Text

For Whom: Audience   Context: When and Where

Whether reading the Homeric poetry in the fifth century BCE or reading the Bible in the twenty-first century CE, Aristotle's observation remains true. In order to understand the rhetorical experience of reading a text interpretation must take into account all three characters—the speaker, the speech, and the audience. Accordingly, reading the New Testament resembles more a lively discussion among students in a theological seminar than a solitary student writing a theological essay in a quiet corner of the library. A seminar features structured conversation which aims toward deeper and fuller understanding. The discussion is frequently messy and open-ended. The conversation partners share hunches about the meaning and significance of the text under discussion. They challenge one another's interpretative proposals. The discourse partners argue, critique, and revise their readings of the text. They may rethink old thoughts. They may dig in their heels and hold on to vested interests. But it is also possible that minds may be changed. It is not possible to determine ahead of time what will happen to the discourse partners as they take up the writings of the New Testament. The promise of the discourse is that new vistas on familiar readings may be opened up. If genuine engagement has taken place, participants will not be left as they were when they began. Even as the individual classroom session draws to a close the matters under consideration, likely, will not have been answered once and for all. Encounter with the Bible is like the lively, dynamic engagement with other people as we move together through the changes and chances of life. Each of us participates as both speaker and hearer.

By Whom: The Speaker

Whether a television advertisement commending the effectiveness of a particular pain reliever or the biblical claim that Jesus is the way, the truth, and the life, the audience wants to know who says so. What basis and qualifications does the speaker have for making this particular claim? What vested interests does the speaker have in the claim? From what experiential perspective does the speaker make the claim? Does the speaker have a reputation for reliability? As an audience on the receiving end of any communication we want to know: Who says so?

Answering the question will prove complex. Just because a televised spokesperson for a particular pain remedy wears a white lab coat does not necessarily mean that the person is a doctor. But even if the spokesperson is an actor playing the part of a doctor, it does not necessarily mean that the claim is untrue. Discerning the truth in television advertising requires awareness and effort on the part of the audience. Untangling the relationship between the biblical authors and the message of the New Testament text demands at least as much effort.

A rhetorical approach to the question provides a path to the truth of the New Testament that helps to keep us from falling off into the ditches on either side. On the one side runs the ditch of blind skepticism; on the other side, the ditch of blind faith. On the surface, blind faith and blind skepticism may seem very different ways of dealing with the question of truth. But scratch the surface and they begin to appear more alike than one might at first imagine. After all, what is the difference? Blind faith says, "No solid basis exists for knowing the truth of God; you just have to believe." Blind skepticism says, "No solid basis for knowing the truth of God exists; you can't just believe." Both approaches to theological truth assume that there is no foundation sufficiently solid to sustain faith in the promise of the biblical God. The experience of the writers of the New Testament calls that assumption into question. In Jesus of Nazareth they encountered the irresistible promise of God which they found compellingly trustworthy. As the Gospel writer John declares, "Jesus, the way, the truth, and the life!" Are we justified to put our faith in the promise of Jesus to give life? A rhetorical approach to the question wants to know three things: 1) Who is making the promise (speaker)? 2) What is being promised (speech)? 3) Who are we to put our faith in the promise (audience)? So then, as to the first question: Whose voice do we hear when reading the New Testament? Who is speaking?

Answering the question will require sorting out the variety of voices with which contemporary students must contend in the encounter with the New Testament writings. There are four possibilities: 1) the historical author, 2) the "implied author," 3) the narrator, and 4) the interpreter / reader. Let's flesh out the promise and problem of the four possibilities.

1) We might be inclined to answer that in the encounter with the New Testament writings we hear the voice of the historical author. Some biblical scholars seek even to establish the "message" of the New Testament by referring to the intention of the historical author. But access to historical authors and their intentions is not without problems. 2) More sophisticated students of historical literature suggest that we may be on firmer ground by identifying the speaker as the **"implied author."**[3] 3) Literary scholars argue that in fact what readers of any literature, including the literature of the New Testament, hear is the voice of the **narrator**. And this cannot be denied. But neither could it

---

[3]"Implied author" may be an unfamiliar term to students in their first university course on reading the New Testament. In the ensuing paragraphs we will develop the designation and its significance for the encounter with the New Testament writings.

be denied that the narrator has no voice until readers give it voice. In that sense the speaker of the New Testament is the contemporary reader. As you can see, with the question of the speaker we have some sorting out to do. 4) Students soon learn that however we imagine the speaker, hearing the voice of the New Testament involves interpretation. What contemporary readers of the New Testament hear will depend on how the material is interpreted and performed. Thus there is the interpreter's voice to contend with.

The Historical Author

As a historical question about the original authors of the New Testament materials, the question of the speaker is not only difficult, but in most cases impossible to answer. With the exception of the writings of Paul, the authors of the New Testament are unknown to us. Sources from the second century ascribe authorial names—Matthew, Mark, Luke, and John—to the Gospels. Scholars, however, for a variety of reasons, do not consider the tradition to be reliable. We can be certain that apart from Paul's letters, the works of the New Testament, in most cases, bear no internal indication of who wrote them. Even in the instances where the writings of the New Testament do contain internal identification of the author we can know very little about the person. In other words, in most cases it is impossible to connect the writings of the New Testament to specific historical persons. This means that the integrity and authority of the writings cannot be derived from the integrity and authority of their authors. Similarly, the aim of the New Testament writings cannot be established on the basis of the author's intention. Contemporary readers simply do not have access to the intentions of the New Testament authors. If you have a question about something that I have written in this introduction you can ask and I can tell you what I intended. In the classroom I am available to you in just that way. The authors of the New Testament, however, even if we knew who they were, are not available to answer questions about what they intended.

The "Implied Author"

History may provide no means, or little means, by which to associate the New Testament materials with specific historical persons. It does not imply, however, that readers can know nothing about these authors. We can know the "character" of the New Testament authors from their works, from what they tell and how they tell it. Literary scholars call this "character" the "implied author." An example will help to clarify the meaning. Donald Juel points out that history provides no access to the actual author of Mark's Gospel. Historical considerations lead us to doubt the tradition that identifies Mark, the secretary and traveling companion of the Apostle Peter, as the author of the Second Gospel. That does not leave the reader completely in the dark however. Inferences may be drawn from the story to develop a portrait of the author. For example, the author tells the story from the point of view of a believer. As the first verse announces, the author regards the story as the beginning of the good news of Jesus, the Messiah, the Son of God. Furthermore, the textual evidence indicates that the author tells the story in the ordinary language of the street, not in refined literary prose. The story also evidences familiarity with the Jewish Scriptures as well as familiarity with Jewish customs, symbols, and traditions. Additionally, the author demonstrates facility with narrative strategies of the day. From these features of the Markan text interpretation can hypothesize that the author was an ordinary Jewish follower of Jesus. While his command of Greek may have been quite rudimentary nonetheless he demonstrates a sophisticated and artful capacity as a storyteller. This way of fleshing out the "implied author" of Mark's Gospel also applies to the other writings of the New Testament. Each provides clues that enable readers to flesh out the "character" of the author on the basis of what they tell and how they tell it.

The Narrator

Actually, literary scholars point out that in any piece of literature there are three speakers. In addition to the actual author and the implied author, there is also the narrator. It is, in fact, the voice of the narrator that speaks in the telling of a story. Robert Fowler pictures what we are saying in this way:[4]

Speaker: Actual Author ⟹ Implied Author ⟹ **Narrator** ⟹ Text

Hearing the voice of the narrator is somewhat tricky because in reality, as we acknowledged above, readers themselves give voice to the narrator. A more accurate picture of "the voice of the speaker" would be:

Speaker: Actual Author ⟹ Implied Author ⟹ Narrator ⟹ **Reader** ⟹ Text

Readers tend to give voice to the narrator without much, if any, thought to how the narrative voice should sound. A rhetorical approach focuses attention on the considerations that are taken into account or should be taken into account as readers embody the voice of the narrator.

Many years ago, when I was a seminary student, we were taught that, when reading aloud for an audience, the Bible should always be read in a monotone voice, head down, no facial expression or body language in evidence. The idea was that the reading should not affect the hearer's reception of the text. However, should readers heed the advice, hearers would likely experience the Bible in an unintended way, namely, as the most boring book in the world. A text cannot be read—aloud or silently—without giving interpretative expression to the reading. One way or another, readers give expression to the voice of the narrator. The real question is how should the voice of the narrator sound? Should it sound like the voice that reads the evening news? Should it sound like the voice of a television evangelist from the Bible Belt? Would the voice of a hip-hop artist be

---

[4]See Robert Fowler, *Let the Reader Understand* (Minneapolis: Fortress Press, 1991), 31ff.

appropriate? Part of the answer to such questions will lie in the determination of what the story should do to hearers. Should the telling comfort or disturb? Should it offer affirmation or should it call into question long-held convictions? A rhetorical approach to interpretation opens up for consideration reasons for reading in a particular way.

Of course readers are not at complete liberty to make such decisions. While the New Testament does not provide explicit "stage directions" for the voice of the narrator, the text does offer data that bear upon such questions. Like all characters in the story the narrator is the creation of the author. The narrator may be a participant in the reported events or an observer. He or she may speak from a limited point of view or an omniscient point of view. The report of the narrator may be reliable or unreliable. Determination of the narrative point of view can only be made on the basis of clues in the text itself. Interpretation from a rhetorical point of view aims to collect and process the relevant data of the text in order that readers may give voice to the narrator in a faithful and effective way.

The way in which the data is processed and comes to voice in a particular reading of the biblical text will disclose not only the "character" of the narrator in the story but also the "character" of the reader of the story as well. There are two reasons for this: 1) While the biblical text provides clues from which to give voice to the narrator, how the clues are processed actually takes place in the imagination of readers. 2) The imagination of readers is not objectively neutral, but operates with preconceived notions that have been shaped by previous readings of the Bible, by experiences in life, and by theological convictions. By way of illustration let me propose a little experiment. Open your Bible to Mark's story of Jesus's crucifixion—Mark 15:33–39. Our focus is on the response of the centurion to the death of Jesus: "Now when the centurion, who stood facing [Jesus], saw that in this way he breathed his last, he said, 'Truly this man was God's Son'" (v. 39). Our experiment poses the question, "How should the narrator represent the voice of the centurion?" Most readers will automatically answer that the centurion speaks sincerely. He sees something in the death of Jesus that makes him a believer. He sees Jesus for whom he is, "Truly this man was God's Son." Whether in private or public readings the voice of the centurion has almost always been read to sound sincere.

But why read the words of the centurion as a sincere confession of faith? What basis does the story provide to suggest that the centurion's confession is sincere? Why not read it as sarcastic ridicule of Jesus and those who believe him to be God's Son: "Yeah, right, truly, this man was God's Son. What a joke!"? Such a reading would be consistent with the attitude of the soldiers up to this point in the story. In fact Jesus and belief in him as the Son of God has been ridiculed by practically all the characters in the story—"all those who passed by derided him (15:29) . . . In the same way the chief priests, along with the scribes, were also mocking him (15:31) . . . [even] those who were crucified with him also taunted him (15:32). And earlier in the story the soldiers had made a mockery of him and the claim that he was "King of the Jews" (15:16–20). Why not read the centurion's response to the death of Jesus as one more, final insult to him and to faith? On the basis of the textual evidence readers could make a good case for such a reading. The interesting question is what affect would such a reading of the story have on hearers today?

A rhetorical approach not only takes an interest in deciding how the text of the New Testament should be given voice, but as well it considers how and why hearers respond to a particular reading. What do hearers find attractive and comforting or disturbing and resistive? What insights to the life of faith do particular readings offer? For example, why would readers prefer one reading over the other? How does it affect the way that the story plays if the centurion speaks sincerely? How does it play if he speaks sarcastically? My experience has been that most prefer to hear the voice of the centurion as a sincere confession of faith. Why? Why do hearers resist reading the words of the centurion as sarcasm? In our world, in the world in front of the Markan text, there are believers and there are those who ridicule faith. Why not also in Mark's world? What if the centurion's ridicule of Jesus unwittingly tells the truth about Jesus as Mark knows it? What does it say about God and the life of faith if those who intentionally ridicule faith, ironically, speak the truth? The Apostle Paul knew exactly what to make of it. As he declared to the Corinthian Christians: "Has not God made foolish the wisdom of the world? . . . We proclaim Christ crucified, a stumbling block to Jews and foolishness to Gentiles, but to those who are the called, both Jews and Greeks, Christ the power of God and the wisdom of God" (1 Cor. 1:20, 22–24).

Of course there is nothing specific in the Markan text at verse 39 to determine which way the claim of the centurion is to be taken—sincerely or sarcastically? A rhetorical approach seeks to uncover what moves readers to take the centurion's words in the one way or the other. A rhetorical approach presumes that reading the Bible not only shows God to readers, but reading the Bible also shows readers to themselves as they are seen by God. Reading the part of the narrator compels us to reveal how we "play" our parts in the drama of God and humanity. A rhetorical approach is less concerned with establishing the one correct way of reading and more concerned with what happens to readers in the encounter with particular readings.

This is not to suggest that there is no specific content to the Bible. Nor is it to suggest that readers are at complete liberty to make of the Bible whatever they wish. The text itself, or according to Aristotle's terminology, the "speech" of the text imposes constraints on how readers make out the message. To this aspect of things we turn when we take up the New Testament as the speech of God. But first we turn to the question of audience.

For Whom: The Audience

As Aristotle pointed out, texts are written for an audience. We have posed the question of audience by asking, "Who are *we* to hear and engage the New Testament?" It could perhaps go without saying that we are as diverse as we appear to be in physical appearance. Our diversity runs deeper than physical appearances of course. We are comprised of diverse backgrounds, experiences, interests, convictions, aspirations, orientations, loyalties, hopes, hurts, fears, likes, and dislikes. This much seems evident from the outset, to suppose a generic homogeneous audience for the New Testament would be a fiction that does not match reality. The audience of the New Testament is always a diverse group of particular flesh and blood people. No doubt our diversity explains why we hear and respond to the New Testament in different ways. Individual audience members hear the writings of the New Testament through the filter of the communities and cultures to which they belong. Many factors—personal experiences and convictions; social, economic, and political position; gender; vested interests; and so on—influence how we hear the New Testament.

It cannot be denied that getting the message of the New Testament is as much a function of what audiences get out of a text, as it is what authors put into the text. But readers are not merely taken and left as they are. Stories work to create and shape their audience. Since the days of Homer successful authors appreciate that stories are only as good as their audiences. What good is a story if it does not engage its audience? A rhetorical approach seeks to understand how readers become an engaged audience. It seeks to appreciate how literary works reshape their audiences. Or we might even go so far as to say a rhetorical approach to the New Testament seeks to appreciate how the New Testament constructs a community of faith in God's promise. As the Fourth Evangelist declares, the aim of telling the story of Jesus is that readers "may come to believe that Jesus is the Messiah, the Son of God, and that through believing you may have life in his name" (John 20:31).

When and Where: The Audience in Theological Context

Listening to the story of the New Testament may reveal that despite all our differences we may have more in common than we might imagine. Take for example the New Testament story in which Jesus declares the good news, "If you continue in my word . . . you will know the truth, and the truth will make you free" (John 8:31–32). Contemporary audiences are bound to respond in the very same way that Jesus's narrative audience responds, "We . . . have never been slaves to anyone. What do you mean by saying, 'You will be made free'?" (John 8:33). As Luther has said, the encounter with the biblical story reveals that the human being is bound to defend its self-proclaimed freedom. We are bound to deny our bondage to defending our freedom at all costs. "So they picked up stones to throw at him" (John 8:59).

Popularly the most common strategy for getting "into" a story is to identify with the characters in the story. This for example is what seems to Ignatius the most promising and consequential way into the world of the New Testament. As he advises in the *Spiritual Exercises,* entering into the biblical story of faith one seeks to "see with the sight of the imagination, the synagogues, villages and towns"[5] in which Jesus once-upon-a-time kicked dust. Readers seek to imagine themselves in the story world of the narrative. Ignatius is not alone in suggesting such an approach to engagement with the Bible. Preachers and teachers of all traditions have encouraged such a view. They encourage the mem-

---

[5]Ignatius of Loyola, *The Spiritual Exercises*. Edited by David L. Fleming (St. Louis: The Institute of Jesuit Sources, 1978), 64.

bers of their "audience" to consider how they are like doubting Thomas, Impetuous Peter, Judas the betrayer, and so on. As commonplace as such a strategy may be, it offers, however, only a limited possibility of engagement. The difficulty with such an approach is the narratives themselves. They make it virtually impossible for readers to identify with the characters in the story. The narratives draw some characters in negative terms. It is not likely that readers will identify with them. Despite the best effort of preachers and other moralists to convince hearers that they are more like the "judgmental Pharisees" of the story than they might ever care to admit, nonetheless readers are not likely to identify with them. Even when characters are drawn more sympathetically readers have difficulty identifying with them. The problem is that readers know too much to identify with the characters in the story. And that is not accidental. Consider the perspective of the reader in Mark's story of Jesus as an example. To the human characters in the story the identity of Jesus is a mystery. For various reasons the human characters seem unable to put two and two together. As the disciples ask of Jesus after he rescues them from the fearsome storm at sea, "Who then can this be that even wind and sea obey him?" (Mark 4:41). To readers of the story there is no mystery about it. Jesus's activities only confirm what they have known from the very beginning of the story. Far from identifying with the bewildered confusion of the characters in the story, readers on the basis of what they know are inclined to answer the question of the disciples: "Wake up and smell the coffee! Who could this be that even sea and wind obey him? How many possibilities are there?" In other words, readers are put in the position of an audience for whose sake the drama plays out. What actual audiences make of the drama cannot be determined apart from actual interpretative proposals. Thus, for a rhetorical approach, the central question of interpretation concerns, "What counts as a good reason for reading and responding to the story in a particular way?" The question keeps interpretation in all its aspects firmly fixed on the readers to account for their response to the narratives.

A rhetorical approach takes for granted that literature, including the literature of the New Testament, is written to be heard by an audience. Ultimately rhetorical interpretation concerns what listeners hear and how they are affected by the whole experience of the story. In this regard the challenge of interpretation is to hear the individual parts in light of the whole and the whole in light of the individual parts.

A rhetorical approach to the study of the New Testament asks what must an audience—any audience, modern or ancient—know in order to make sense of the text. In other words, who is the implied audience and what must it know to find the text engaging on its own terms? For example, readers of the Gospels, if they are to make sense of the story, are expected to be familiar with the geo-political lay of Palestine. Where is Galilee and what is its reputation? Further, readers must have some knowledge of the socio-political makeup of the Jewish community. Who are the Pharisees, Sadducees, Zealots, and Herodians? What is their place in society and what are the beliefs that characterize them? Readers are expected to be familiar with historic figures. Who is Pontius Pilate and how does he play into the story? Readers are expected to be familiar with certain titles. What does it mean to name Jesus as Messiah of Israel? Contemporary readers may never know enough to put themselves fully in the sandals of the original audience but historical investigation promises to uncover answers by which contemporary audiences may more fruitfully engage with the text of the New Testament. What listeners hear and how they respond to it is the conversation that makes the whole enterprise worthwhile, particularly at the point of its consequence for the human encounter with God.

What: The Text and Message of the New Testament as Speech of God

Thus far in our introduction to reading the New Testament we have shown that both literary and historical approaches to the material are indispensable. Both enrich the reader's encounter with the message. Particularly as we proceed now to bring more sharply into focus the relationship between the ancient literature of the New Testament and its message for today we have occasion to appreciate complementarity of our three approaches and the overarching importance of the rhetorical approach.

© 2012 JupiterImages Corp.

If interpretation were to take only a historical approach to the study of the New Testament materials it might leave the impression that the message of the New Testament is to be located in the past. The historical imagination has frequently operated with the paradigm of then and now. The message is determined and applied to the present-tense "now" on the basis of what the text meant "then," in the ancient context. The focus of inquiry is on what the ancient author intended and/or what the text meant to the original readers. We have sought to show that such an approach is inadequate and misleading for at least two reasons. First, the search for ancient authors and audiences has proven allusive and thus an unstable ground on which to determine the message of the text. Second, even if it were possible to determine the message of the New Testament on the basis of the way it was understood by an ancient audience it would leave present-day readers with a message that was meant for another time and place. While historical study cannot determine the message of the New Testament for present-day readers nonetheless it is useful. It expands our background knowledge in ways that make us better readers and more appreciative of the message.

Similarly, a literary approach to the writings of the New Testament is indispensable to an encounter with the message. The New Testament message does not exist apart from its literary expression. Thus all the considerations that come into play in making sense of words on the page apply in the interpretation of the New Testament message for today—genre, philology, grammar, point of view, and so forth. However, if interpretation were to operate solely with a literary approach it might leave the impression that interpretation involves uncovering the message hidden in the text. Frequently interpretation has taken exactly this approach to the parables of Jesus. Interpretation views the New Testament, especially the parables of Jesus, as equivalent to Aesop's Fables. The premise is that the parables contain a "lesson." Interpretation aims to extract and apply the "lesson" to life today. Such a reading offers only a limited engagement with the message.

A rhetorical approach views the literature of the New Testament less like a container in which authors hide their message. Rather, a rhetorical approach regards literature as a force, mightier than the sword. It views the New Testament not only as a message about God, but as the very speech of God. The Fourth Evangelist writes the story of Jesus so that readers may encounter the same life-giving word of God that people encountered in Jesus. In Jesus people, including the author of the Fourth Gospel, encountered the grace and truth of God which gives life to the world: "And the Word [of God] became flesh and lived among us, and we have seen his glory, the glory as of a father's only son, full of grace and truth" (John 1:14). Jesus does not come with a message about God, but comes as the living speech of God. Ironically as it turns out not everyone has an ear for the promise of God as Jesus speaks it: "He came to his own and his own people did not accept him. But to all who received him, who believed in his name, he gave power to become children of God, who were born, not of blood or of the will of the flesh or of the will of man, but of God" (John 1:11–13). It cannot be determined ahead of time what will become of the reader in relation to God. Will the reader encounter the grace and truth of God? Only the actual encounter will determine the outcome. In the final analysis the outcome of the encounter may depend more on God than on interpreters. As Jesus says flat out in the course of John's story, "no one can come to me unless it is granted by the Father" (John 6:65). Or as Jesus explains to the religious leader, Nicodemus, "no one can see the kingdom of God without being born from above" (John 3:3). So while it cannot be said ahead of time what will become of readers in the encounter there is promise. As Jesus declared, "I will not leave you orphaned. I will send the Spirit of Truth who will lead you into all truth" (John 14).

Getting in Touch with the Rhetoric of the New Testament

Now that we have definition and description of a rhetorical approach to interpretation we need to think together in pragmatic terms about the implications for interpretation. If you have ever found yourself thinking about body language, tone of voice, word choice, or searching for clues to understand why someone said this or that to you, then you have done rhetorical analysis. A rhetorical approach to the New

Testament is similar. Rhetorical analysis applies critical reading skills to break down the "whole" of the text into the sum of its "parts." It seeks to understand and make clear how the New Testament and its interpretation functions to shape our theological understanding, and how in fact the New Testament shapes us as human beings. The rhetorical triangle brings into focus the primary considerations which illuminate the rhetoric of the New Testament. Using the rhetorical triangle, interpreters ask the following questions:

Of the Speaker:

–Who is the speaker and what type of speaker is he or she?

–What stance is he or she taking?

–What are his or her beliefs, values, and assumptions?

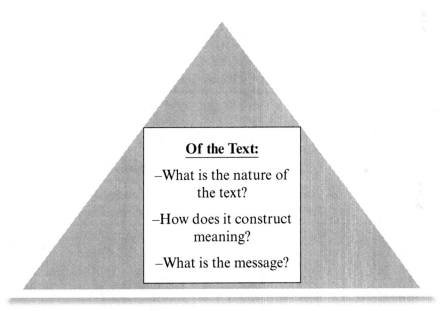

Of the Text:

–What is the nature of the text?

–How does it construct meaning?

–What is the message?

Of the Audience:

–To whom is the speech addressed?

–What is the purpose?

–Does the speech presume or create an audience?

–What is the position of the audience in relation to the events of the narrative?

–What must the audience know to make sense of the speech?

Of the Context:

–How does the speech "play" in the World Behind the Text / In Front of the Text?

Evaluating Sound Arguments Today

At the outset of this chapter we said that a rhetorical approach to interpretation concerns making arguments for particular ways of reading a text. Interpretative discussion that promises to lead to deeper and more profound "readings" of the biblical text requires, therefore, a means of evaluating theological arguments. **PARIS**—city of love, but also city of Enlightenment serves nicely as an acronym for the elements which comprise the analysis of arguments (logos). The considerations highlighted in the table below overlap one another to some extent. The table seeks to identify individual considerations that help to evaluate the strength and adequacy of arguments.

P	Presuppositions	What foundational ideas does the argument presuppose? What givens does it take for granted? Are these "presuppositions" accurate and true? How do or can we know?
A	Assumptions	What assumptions are made about experience in the real world? Are the assumptions true and accurate? What is the context (historical and cultural) of the argument?
R	Relations	How do the ideas in this argument relate to other ideas which seem also to be true? Does it take into account other points of view?
I	Implications	Where does this argument lead us? If true, what does it imply about the proper way to live and believe?
S	Sufficiency	How well does it take account of reality as we experience it? Does it ignore or misconstrue any data of our experience?

Terms:

Rhetoric	Pathos
Rhetorical Triangle	Logos
Ethos	PARIS

Study Questions:

1. Describe Aristotle's understanding of: 1) pathos, 2) logos, and 3) ethos. How do they relate to the study of the New Testament?

2. What is the "rhetorical triangle" and how does it relate to the study of the New Testament?

3. What is the aim of rhetorical analysis?

4. How does rhetorical analysis apply to the New Testament?

For Further Study:

Ellen F. Davis and Richard B. Hays, editors. *The Art of Reading Scripture.* Grand Rapids: Eerdmans' Publishing Company, 2003. Catholic and Protestant scholars address the question of reading the Bible as the Scriptures of the Christian church.

Beverly Gaventa and Patrick Miller. *The Ending of Mark and the Ends of God: Essay in Memory of Donald Harrisville Juel.* Louisville: Westminster John Knox Press, 2005. This collection of essays in memory of Don Juel argues in a variety of ways that the Bible itself resists any and all attempts to domesticate its message. Or perhaps better to say that these essays argue that the God of the Bible resists all interpretative attempts to domesticate him.

Donald Juel. *Shaping the Scriptural Imagination: Truth, Meaning, and the Theological Interpretation of the Bible.* Edited by Shane Berg and Matthew L. Skinner. Waco: Baylor University Press, 2011. Former students edit with commentary previously unpublished essays of Donald Juel. Juel's concern was to understand what happens, and should happen, when people read the Bible. How is God present or made known in the act of reading?

Appendix **A**

Glossary of Terms

Alexander the Great. (356–323 BCE). Macedonian military leader who established the influence of Greek ways (Hellenism) throughout the eastern Mediterranean region.

Antichrist. The arch enemy of God who leads the forces of evil in battle against God.

Apocalypse. A literary genre which employs myth and symbolism to portray God's purposes in leading history to its intended culmination. The vision is delivered from a heavenly agent to a human agent on behalf of the audience.

Apocalyptic theology. Divides time and reality into two realms, the temporal realm which is controlled by the forces of evil, and the eschatological kingdom of God which will eventually displace and defeat worldly evil.

Apologetics. A reasoned explanation of and justification for a set of beliefs, usually set forth in the frame of reference of the discourse partners.

Aristotle. Influential philosopher of Greece during the fifth century BC. Student of Plato. Tutor of Alexander the Great. His writings cover many subjects, including physics, metaphysics, poetry, theater, music, logic, rhetoric, linguistics, politics, government, ethics, biology, and zoology.

Apostle. From a Greek word meaning sent with the full authority of the sender. In the New Testament it designates emissaries of Jesus.

Asclepius. God of the Greek pantheon, noted for health and healing.

Autograph. An original manuscript of a literary text.

Baptism. The rite of entrance into the Christian community. The sacramental means by which God claims an individual as his own and promises to fulfill the First Commandment to and for the baptismal recipient.

BC / AD. System of dating and dividing time on the basis of the life of Jesus. BC indicates the time prior to Jesus and AD refers to the years following the time of Jesus, literally, *anno domini*. See below, the entry on BCE and CE for an alternative system of dating.

BCE / CE. System of dating roughly corresponding to the Christian system which utilizes BC (Before Christ) and AD (*anno domini*, in the year of our Lord). Some scholars prefer it because it seems to them more neutral than the Christian designations.

Bible. Literally, book of books or library of books. The most common way to refer to the Christian scriptures. It draws attention to the collection consisting of many books composed over centuries.

Canon. Literally refers to a measuring rod. Used to designate the biblical writings as the Scriptures of the Christian church, writings considered to bring forth the normative and authoritative understanding of God and humans in relation to one another.

Catholic. A term which signifies universal. Used in reference to the general epistles of the New Testament: 1 and 2 Peter, James, Jude, 1, 2, 3 John, and Hebrews.

Chief priests. Jewish religious leaders who presided over the affairs of the Temple in Jerusalem and members of the Sanhedrin, the Jewish "Supreme Court."

Christ. Greek version of Hebrew Messiah. The special king who according to the promise of God, would arise from the household of David to restore the fortunes of Israel and establish God's rule in undisputed fashion over all creation (see, e.g., 2 Sam. 7:7ff).

Christian Scriptures. A designation for the Bible that brings into focus their foundational, normative, and authoritative function within the community of faith.

Christology. Theological understanding of Jesus and his significance for faith, or for the human relationship to God.

Constantine. Fourth-century emperor of the Roman Empire who established Christianity as the religion of the Roman realm.

Covenant. Agreement between two parties, used to characterize the relationship between God and Israel. The Jewish scriptures speak of a variety of covenants, mediated by heroes of the faith—Abraham, Moses, and David. In each case the agreement stated that God would protect and preserve the people so long as they remained obedient to the law of God. The prophet Jeremiah promises a new covenant when devotion and obedience will be written on the heart of faithful Israel (Jer. 31:31–34).

Dead Sea Scrolls. A library of Jewish literature from the first century consisting of commentaries on the Jewish Scriptures, community rules, and so forth. Associated with the community at Qumran, sometimes known as the Essenes.

Deutero-Pauline Epistles. A designation for three letters of Paul regarded by the majority opinion of scholars to be written after Paul's death by a colleague or student to represent the Apostle's thought in an unprecedented situation—2 Thessalonians, Ephesians, and Colossians.

Diaspora. A Greek term that literally means dispersion. Used to reference the community of Jews who were compelled to live outside Palestine.

Diatribe. A form of Greek argumentation. The term means literally to lead along the way. Paul adopts this form of argument to lead his conversation partners from his thesis along the way answering objections and questions to the conclusion.

Disciple. Identifies a follower of Jesus as a student.

Epistle. Synonym of letter.

Eschatology. Names the theological field of study that focuses attention on the ultimate aims of God.

Essenes. A community of Jews who withdrew into the wilderness to live a life of purity in preparation for the final battle of God against evil. Sometimes referred to as the community of Qumran. Generally believed to have produced the literature known as the Dead Sea Scrolls.

Eusebius. Fourth-century Christian historian who chronicled the Christian movement from its beginning to the time of Constantine. An essential source of information about Christian origins.

Evangelist. In biblical studies, used to name the authors of the Gospels which tell the story of Jesus for faith.

Exercitants. Name for those who undertake Ignatius's spiritual exercises.

Exegesis. Refers to the process and rules for reading and interpreting the Bible.

Feminist Criticism. An approach to reading the Bible from the point of view of women's experience in the world and which promotes liberation of women in contemporary church and society.

Galilee. The northern province of Israel.

Gematria. An ancient form of Jewish and Greek interpretation based on the numerical value of letters and words.

Genre. Synonymous with type of literature. The New Testament essentially contains three types of literature—narratives, letters, and apocalypse.

Gentiles. A generic Jewish designation for non-Jews.

Gospel. When it appears in upper case it designates narrative writings of the New Testament that tell the story of Jesus and his significance for faith. When it appears in lower case it designates the Christian message, the good news of Jesus.

Hebrew Bible. Designation for the Jewish Scriptures, preferred by scholars because it is perceived to be more neutral.

Hellenism. The spread of Greek language and culture throughout the Mediterranean world.

Heresy. Deviation from established normative beliefs.

Hermeneutic of suspicion. An approach to reading the Bible that seeks to uncover hidden agendas and vested interests.

Hermeneutics. The process and rules of interpretation.

Herodians. A small group of Jewish aristocrats associated with the court of King Herod.

Herod the Great. King of Israel, appointed by the occupational rule of Rome, from 37–4 BCE.

Historical-Critical Method. A method of studying the biblical literature which seeks to understand the writings in the historical milieu of their origin.

Historicity. References events of the narrative that actually took place in the world of real time.

Idol. Literally means an empty reality, used by Christians and Jews to indicate false gods.

Implied Author. The author of a piece as he or she can be made out from what is told and how it is told.

Implied Reader. The reader of a piece as he or she is shaped by the piece itself. Sometimes referred to as the ideal reader.

Intercalation. Weaving two narrative strands together in a way that they mutually interpret one another.

Interlocutor. Conversation partner.

Josephus. A first-century Jewish historian in the court of the Emperor Vespasian. An essential source of information about the New Testament era.

Judea. Southern province of Israel.

Justification by Faith. The biblical doctrine that humans exist in a right relationship to God by trusting God's promise to be God for them.

Law. Conditional word of God to establish and maintain order in the creation and by which humans are held accountable to God.

Lection. Indicates a select portion of biblical text. Synonymous with pericope.

Lectionary. Systematic schedule of reading selected passages of the Bible in the public worship of the church.

Letter. Synonym for epistle, one division of literature within the New Testament.

Literary-Critical Method. A method of interpreting the biblical literature which seeks to understand the Bible as literature.

Manuscript. Physical copy of a literary text. In the case of the biblical literature usually hand-written.

Messiah. From a Hebrew word that means, anointed one. In biblical literature it names the special King who God promised to David from David's family who would establish forever after undisputed the rule of God over all creation (see 2 Sam. 7:7–9).

Millennium. Thousand-year reign of Christ on earth. In the Book of Revelation the designation does not function literally to locate the reign of Christ in a particular time. Rather, it functions symbolically to suggest the victorious rule of God over opposing forces.

Metaphysics. The branch of philosophy that concerns how reality coheres in the big picture.

Method. Literally, the "road into." Used to designate the disciplined approaches to the study of the Bible.

Mishnah. Teaching tradition of the Rabbis. Initially passed orally from generation to generation and eventually written down around 200 CE.

Narrative. Literary form consisting of plot, character, and setting. Events are related in such a way so as to show their connection.

Myth. A story which tells/relates a reality that is always and everywhere true.

Pantheon. Greek and Roman gods taken as a group.

Parable. Form of Jesus's teaching which employs a story to illustrate some aspect of the kingdom of God.

Passion Narrative. The story of Jesus's arrest, trial, and execution.

Passover. Annual festival of Jews celebrating their exodus from Egyptian slavery and their formation as the people of God.

Pastoral Epistles. Three letters—Titus, 1 and 2 Timothy—bearing the name of Paul, but written by a colleague or student after his death to represent his teaching about church leadership.

Pauline Corpus. The collection of all the New Testament writings bearing the name of Paul.

Pericope. Indicates a select portion of biblical text. Synonymous with lection.

Pharisees. A lay renewal movement with Judaism of the first century that emphasized the importance of the law in leading a truly Jewish life.

Philo. A Jewish teacher of the first century who sought to understand Jewish tradition in Greek categories.

Plato. A Greek philosopher who made defining contributions to the Greek understanding of theology.

Pre-understanding. The knowledge, attitudes, and experiences that one brings to reading the Bible.

Primary Sources. Historical term which indicates literary artifacts contemporaneous with the period under investigation to reconstruct the era. They are two kinds: voluntary (written for the same of prosperity) and involuntary (written to address a circumstance within the era).

Prophet. A person who speaks the truth of God. Also designates the third major division of writings that comprise the Jewish Scriptures.

Pseudonymity. The widely accepted practice of antiquity by which an author wrote under the name of the person whose thought they sought to represent.

Q. Designation for the unknown source that Matthew and Luke purportedly used in the composition of their Gospels.

Qumran. Community of Jewish aesthetics who withdrew from the corruption of urban life to the purity of the wilderness as they awaited and prepared for the final assault of God against his evil enemies.

Rhetor. One who employs persuasive conventions and strategies in setting forth an argument.

Rhetorical Criticism. A field of biblical interpretation that focuses attention on the capacity of the biblical literature to create and move audiences.

Rhetorical Triangle. A means of considering the place of author, audience, and context in the examination of how literature functions to create and shape reader/hearers.

Sadducees. A first-century Jewish sect whose base of power was associated with the Temple in Jerusalem. They sought to cooperate with the Roman occupation because they believed that the occupation was God's way of chastening his people.

Samaria. Central province of Israel.

Samaritans. Residents who lived in the central province of Israel. Despised by other Jews because they had intermarried with non-Jews.

Secondary Sources. A historical term to indicate synthesized versions of the past. Designed to bring out the significance of the past events for today.

Second Temple Era. Period of Jewish history from about 520 BCE to 70 CE.

Septuagint. Greek version of the Jewish Scriptures, so named because legend taught that the translation was made by a group of seventy scholars working separately, but whose individual efforts arrived remarkably at the exact same rendering of the Hebrew text in Greek.

Stoicism. School of Greek Philosophy emphasizing self-determination and harmony with the ways of reality.

Synagogue. Though the origin of the institution is obscure it designates house of study; the community center of Jewish life in villages and towns outside Jerusalem.

Synoptic Gospels. The Gospels of Matthew, Mark, and Luke, so named for the scholarly habit of viewing them side-by-side. This way of studying the Gospels led to the compositional theory that Matthew and Luke, writing independently of one another, used Mark and an unknown source (**Q**) in the composition of their Gospels.

Talmud. The Mishnah along with rabbinic commentary, known as Gemarah.

Tanakh. An acronym which names the Jewish Scriptures after the three main divisions of writings—the Torah, the Writings, and the Prophets.

Temple. Located in Jerusalem. The central place of Jewish worship. It was destroyed in 70 CE and never rebuilt.

Testament. Names the divisions of the Bible to designate that the writings tell the truth about God in relation to humanity and humanity in relation to God.

Textual Criticism. The science of sorting, rating, and dating ancient manuscripts for the purpose of reconstructing the original form of the writing.

Textual Data. A term used to focus interpretation on identifying the textual evidence (words on the page, etc.) from which interpretative proposals are developed.

Textual Variants. Different manuscript renderings of the same biblical passage.

Theology. The study of God in relation to creation and creation, including the human creation, in relation to God.

Torah. The law of God, which reveals who God is and who Israel is to be in relation to God. Also one division of the Jewish Scriptures, including the first five books, sometimes referred to as the Books of Moses or the Pentateuch.

Vocation. Calling to some earthly service.

Way. The name used for the Christian community employed principally in Acts. Meaning the way of Jesus.

Writings. The second major division of writings in the Jewish Scriptures which includes the Psalms, Proverbs, and the historical books.

Yahweh. Primary name for God in the Jewish Scriptures. It literally means I am who I am.

Zealots. First-century Jewish sect which sought to overthrow the Roman occupation in the name of Yahweh.

Appendix B
Maps

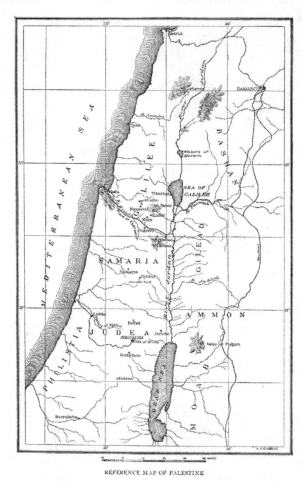

REFERENCE MAP OF PALESTINE

Appendix C

Historical Time Line

For the sake of providing point of reference to students, this time line includes the significant events, people, and literary works that give shape to the historical eras pertinent to understanding the political, social, and cultural world of the Bible. It offers these points of reference in the interest of directing students to relevant research topics as they seek to continue expanding their familiarity with the historical eras related to the production of the biblical materials.

	Events	People	Writers and Writings
10th Century	1000—Davidic Empire God promises a descendent of David to restore fortunes of Israel (2 Sam 7)	Saul, David, Solomon Elijah, and Elisha	
6th Century	587—Babylonian Conquest of Israel, Destruction of the Temple, Exile		
	539—Persian Conquest of Babylon, Edict of Cyrus: Jews are restored to their homeland		
	515—Reconstruction of the Temple begins		
4th Century		Era of Great Greek Philosophers—Socrates, Plato (427–347), Aristotle (384–322), teacher of Alexander the Great	Homeric Poetry committed to written form
	333—Greek Conquest of Persia	323—Death of Alexander the Great, Beginning of Hellenistic Era	

	Events	People	Writers and Writings
2nd Century	Jewish persecutions, religious practices outlawed: circumcision, reading Torah in public, Sabbath observance (168–64) 164–143—Maccabean Revolt (Temple re-consecrated; independent rule restored, Hanukkah)	Rising of Roman Empire	Torah translated into Greek
	104–63—Hasmoneans	Pharisees and Sadducees appear on Jewish scene Essenes establish community at Qumran	Daniel Dead Sea Scrolls
1st Century	63—Roman rule of Palestine Pax Romana	Pompey Julius Caesar (d. 44) Octavian, aka Augustus (from 31)	Philo of Alexandria Virgil

CE	Events	Persons		Writers and Writings
1st Century	6—Census by Quirinius Nero's persecution of Christians during which Paul and Peter are martyred (64–65) Jewish War (66–70) Fall of Jerusalem and Destruction of Temple (70) Jewish rebels take refuge at Masada and commit mass suicide (73) "Rabbinic" Community established in Jamnia by Johanan ben Zakkai Christians expelled from Synagogue (90)	Octavian, aka Augustus (to 14) Tiberius (14–37) Caligula (37–41) Claudius (41–54) Nero (54–68) Galba, Otho, Vitellius (68–69) Vespasian (69–79) Titus (79–81) Domitian (81–96) Nerva (96–98)	Jesus (d. 30?) Pilate (Roman Procurator of Judea, 26–36) Herod the Great (d. 4 / 40-yr rule) Paul (see Chronological Table) Gallio, proconsul in Achaia (51–52)	Oral Tradition (stories and sayings of Jesus transmitted by word of mouth) Letters of Paul (50–60) Mark (70) Matthew (80) Luke–Acts (90) Josephus (90) John (100) Revelation (95) Pastoral Epistles (100)

CE	Events	Persons	Writers and Writings
2nd Century	(132–35) Jewish Revolt led by Bar Kochbah (Proclaimed Messiah by Rabbi Akiba) Jews expelled from Jerusalem	Trajan (98–117) Hadrian (117–138)	Justin Martyr (100–165) Irenaeus (130–202) Clement (150–215) Tertullian (160–240)
3rd Century			Mishnah
4th Century	Christianity becomes religion of the Roman realm Council of Nicaea (325)	Constantine Augustine	Canon of the New Testament published by Bishop Athanasius of Alexandria (367)

Chronology of Paul's Life and Work

We have two sources for dating Paul's life and work. Both sources are canonical: Acts of the Apostles and Paul's own letters. The two sources do not always agree. In fact it is difficult to correlate data from Paul's letters with data from Luke's Acts of the Apostles. For example, Acts divides Paul's missionary work into three distinct phases. There is, however, no indication in the letters of Paul that his missionary endeavors divide into three separate journeys. When dating the life and activities of Paul it seems best to regard the data from Acts as supplemental to the data from Paul's own letters. That is the course that has been followed in developing the chart on the next page.

As with dating events and developments of the Christian movement more generally, dating the events and developments of Paul's life and career in real time is difficult for a number of reasons. The main reason is that in the first century there was no common calendar. At that time people "dated" events in relation to more prevalently known and publicly significant events. Luke for example "dates" the birth of Jesus in relation to the tax census that was taken when Quirinius was governor of Syria (see Luke 2:1). Matthew dates the visit of the magi to the infant Jesus "in the time of King Herod" (Matt. 2:1).

Paul however does not provide many references to public events or persons. So it is difficult to "date" his activities in real time. The one most significant piece of information comes from Acts. In chapter 18 Luke reports that Paul appears before the Roman proconsul, Gallio. On the basis of an inscription at Delphi, historians date Gallio's short tenure in 51–52. Accordingly we presume that Paul was active in establishing congregations of the faith throughout Asia Minor and Greece during the decade of the 50s.

Dates	Activities	Source	Letters
?–32	"Former Life" Model Jew Fulfilled Life Pharisee Zealous for the Law Opponent of "Jewish Christians"	Gal. 1; 2 Cor. 11:16–18; Phil 3:4–11	
32–34	"Conversion"	1 Cor. 15:3–8; Gal. 1; Phil. 3:4–11; Acts 9	
35	First Visit to Jerusalem	Gal. 1:18–19	
35–48	Travels in Syria and Cilicia	Gal. 1:20–24	
48	Second Visit to Jerusalem (Apostolic Conference)	Gal. 2:1–10; Acts 15	
48–?	Apostolic Activity in Asia Minor and Greece Arrest in Jerusalem (58) Martyrdom in Rome (?)	2 Cor. 11;	1 Thessalonians (50) Galatians (54) 1 Corinthians (55) 2 Corinthians (56) Philippians (56) Philemon (56) Romans (57)